# Racialized Bordering Discourses on European Roma

Using detailed examples from Finland, Hungary, Canada and the UK, this book explores relationships between the racialization and discrimination experienced by heterogeneous European Roma populations, and the processes of everyday bordering embedded in state policies and media discourses. In the context of the long histories of discrimination experienced by Roma people across Europe, the chapters engage with changing European Union (EU) policies, including the recent tensions between inter-European de-bordering, rebordering and the selective immigration policies introduced as different states react to EU free movement. Using an intersectional analysis, the authors capture the perspectives of differentially situated people and associated discourses to examine the continuing racism experienced by European Roma citizens in their interaction with bordering technologies. They examine the homogenizing 'racial othering' and construction of Roma as a 'criminal category' that coexists with the differentiations made between 'indigenous' and 'migrant' Roma central to dominant bordering discourses and the contestations of different Roma populations. Chapters focus on Roma activism and the media, the exclusion of Roma residents via urban regeneration and welfare provision, and powerful media and political discourses about Roma populations in different national and transnational contexts.

This book was originally published as a special issue of *Ethnic and Racial Studies*.

**Nira Yuval-Davis** is a Professor and Director of the Centre for Research on Migration, Refugees and Belonging at the University of East London, UK.

**Georgie Wemyss** is Senior Lecturer in Sociology and Co-Director of the Centre for Research on Migration, Refugees and Belonging at the University of East London, UK.

**Kathryn Cassidy** is Senior Lecturer in Human Geography at Northumbria University, UK.

# Ethnic and Racial Studies

Edited by

Martin Bulmer, *University of Surrey, UK*
John Solomos, *University of Warwick, UK*

The journal *Ethnic and Racial Studies* was founded in 1978 by John Stone to provide an international forum for high-quality research on race, ethnicity, nationalism and ethnic conflict. At the time, the study of race and ethnicity was still a relatively marginal subfield of sociology, anthropology and political science. In the intervening period, the journal has provided a space for the discussion of core theoretical issues, key developments and trends, and for the dissemination of the latest empirical research.

It is now the leading journal in its field and has helped to shape the development of scholarly research agendas. *Ethnic and Racial Studies* attracts submissions from scholars in a diverse range of countries and fields of scholarship, and crosses disciplinary boundaries. It is now available in both printed and electronic form. From 2015 it is publishing 15 issues per year, 3 of which are dedicated to *Ethnic and Racial Studies Review* offering expert guidance to the latest research through the publication of book reviews, symposia and discussion pieces, including reviews of work in languages other than English.

The *Ethnic and Racial Studies* book series contains a wide range of the journal's special issues. These special issues are an important contribution to the work of the journal, where leading social science academics bring together articles on specific themes and issues that are linked to the broad intellectual concerns of *Ethnic and Racial Studies*. The series editors work closely with the guest editors of the special issues to ensure that they meet the highest quality standards possible. Through publishing these special issues as a series of books, we hope to allow a wider audience of both scholars and students from across the social science disciplines to engage with the work of *Ethnic and Racial Studies*.

# Racialized Bordering Discourses on European Roma

*Edited by*
**Nira Yuval-Davis, Georgie Wemyss and Kathryn Cassidy**

Routledge
Taylor & Francis Group
LONDON AND NEW YORK

First published 2018
by Routledge

2 Park Square, Milton Park, Abingdon, Oxfordshire OX14 4RN
52 Vanderbilt Avenue, New York, NY 10017

*Routledge is an imprint of the Taylor & Francis Group, an informa business*

First issued in paperback 2019

*British Library Cataloguing in Publication Data*

A catalogue record for this book is available from the British Library

ISBN 13: 978-1-138-29567-4 (hbk)
ISBN 13: 978-0-367-26485-7 (pbk)

Typeset in Myriad Pro
by diacriTech, Chennai

**Publisher's Note**
The publisher accepts responsibility for any inconsistencies that may have arisen
during the conversion of this book from journal articles to book chapters, namely
the possible inclusion of journal terminology.

**Disclaimer**
Every effort has been made to contact copyright holders for their permission to
reprint material in this book. The publishers would be grateful to hear from any
copyright holder who is not here acknowledged and will undertake to rectify any
errors or omissions in future editions of this book.

# Contents

# Citation Information

The chapters in this book were originally published in *Ethnic and Racial Studies*, volume 40, issue 7 (2017). When citing this material, please use the original page numbering for each article, as follows:

**Introduction**
*Introduction to the special issue: racialized bordering discourses on European Roma*
Nira Yuval-Davis, Georgie Wemyss and Kathryn Cassidy
*Ethnic and Racial Studies*, volume 40, issue 7 (2017) pp. 1047–1057

**Chapter 1**
*Follow the money: international donors, external homelands and their effect on Romani media and advocacy*
Shayna Plaut
*Ethnic and Racial Studies*, volume 40, issue 7 (2017) pp. 1058–1076

**Chapter 2**
*Roma communities, urban development and social bordering in the inner city of Budapest*
Krisztina Keresztély, James W. Scott and Tünde Virág
*Ethnic and Racial Studies*, volume 40, issue 7 (2017) pp. 1077–1095

**Chapter 3**
*Media mirrors? Framing Hungarian Romani migration to Canada in Hungarian and Canadian press*
Viktor Varjú and Shayna Plaut
*Ethnic and Racial Studies*, volume 40, issue 7 (2017) pp. 1096–1113

**Chapter 4**
*Coping with everyday bordering: Roma migrants and gatekeepers in Helsinki*
Miika Tervonen and Anca Enache
*Ethnic and Racial Studies*, volume 40, issue 7 (2017) pp. 1114–1131

# CITATION INFORMATION

**Chapter 5**

**Chapter 6**

For any permission-related enquiries please visit:
http://www.tandfonline.com/page/help/permissions

# Notes on Contributors

**Kathryn Cassidy** is Senior Lecturer in Human Geography at Northumbria University, UK.

**Anca Enache** is based at the Department of Finnish, Finno-Ugrian and Scandinavian Studies, University of Helsinki, Finland.

**Mastoureh Fathi** is a Lecturer at the Faculty of Health and Social Sciences, Bournemouth University, UK.

**Jamie Hakim** is a Lecturer in Media Studies at the Department of Media Studies, University of East Anglia, UK.

**Krisztina Keresztély** is based at the Comparative Research Network, Germany.

**Shayna Plaut** is based at the School for International Studies, International Law and Human Security, Simon Fraser University, Canada.

**James W. Scott** is based at the Karelian Institute, University of Eastern Finland, Finland.

**Miika Tervonen** is a postdoctoral researcher at the Department of Social Research, University of Helsinki, Finland.

**Viktor Varjú** is Senior Research Fellow at the Centre for Economic and Regional Studies, Hungarian Academy of Sciences, Hungary.

**Tünde Virág** is a Senior Research Fellow at the Centre for Economic and Regional Studies, Hungarian Academy of Sciences, Hungary.

**Georgie Wemyss** is Senior Lecturer in Sociology and Co-Director of the Centre for Research on Migration, Refugees and Belonging at the University of East London, UK.

**Nira Yuval-Davis** is a Professor and Director of the Centre for Research on Migration, Refugees and Belonging at the University of East London, UK.

# Introduction to the special issue: racialized bordering discourses on European Roma

Nira Yuval-Davis, Georgie Wemyss and Kathryn Cassidy

**ABSTRACT**
In the introduction to this special issue, we briefly introduce everyday bordering as the theoretical framing for the papers and explore its relationship to the process of racialization. We introduce our situated intersectional approach to the study of everyday bordering, illustrating the importance of capturing the differentially situated gazes of a range of social actors. We then go on to contextualize the importance of this framing and approach in a wider discussion of Roma in Europe before concluding with a summary of the particular contributions of each of the papers in this special issue to these debates.

## Racialized bordering discourses on European Roma

We are pleased to introduce this special issue of *Ethnic and Racial Studies* on Roma. Although British and other European racialized discourses have focused primarily on black, southern and increasingly in recent years Muslim minorities, Roma people have continued to be a focus of both racist attitudes and discriminatory policies, in the UK, and in different ways and to varying extents, in other European countries as well as globally. In June 2015, Izsák (2015), the Special Rapporteur for Minority Rights, presented before the Human Rights Council a report on the state of Roma people and "anti-Gypsyism racism" all over the globe. In the announcement about the meeting the Council of Europe defined anti-Gypsyism "as a special kind of racism, an ideology founded on racial supremacy, a form of dehumanization and institutional racism, nurtured by historical discrimination which is expressed by violence, hate speech, exploitation, stigmatisation and the most blatant kind of discrimination".[1]

The articles in this issue focus separately and comparatively on several European countries – specifically Hungary, Finland and the UK – and show the racialized constructions of Roma in Europe. The category and boundaries of the Roma (and related communities such as Romani Gypsies and Travellers) have always been contested (Acton 1997; Hancock 2002; Matras 2002) but in recent years we have seen a growing movement of self-determination encompassing them all, at least nominally, in the European Union (EU) and the United Nations (Feys 1997; Klímová-Alexander 2007) under the umbrella term of Roma. We therefore choose to use this label to include all the hetero-geneous collectivities discussed in this issue.

Special funds and policies aimed at "integrating" and improving the welfare of Roma people have been developed, but at the same time there has been no significant change in the social processes locating them as "Others". After the collapse of the Soviet Union and the enlargement of the EU, differentiation between "indigenous" and migrant Roma began to emerge within racialized discourses towards Roma. In recent populist debates on East European migration to the UK, for example, there has also been a collapse of the categories "Roma" and "Romanians" with a focus on the actions of the former being used to demonize the latter (see Wemyss and Cassidy 2017).

Most of the scholars writing for this issue have been studying the social, economic and political contexts of Roma populations as part of a large Euro-pean research project on EUBorderscapes and everyday bordering.[2] Within the project, the racialized constructions of Roma in media discourses as well as intersectional narratives of everyday social and state borderings, which differentiate, rather than homogenize, different groupings of Roma people, have been the focus of particular strands of the research and analysis.

The first part of this introductory paper focuses on the relationship of racism in general and towards Roma people in particular and intersectional situated constructions of everyday bordering. It then describes in broad brush the history and policies towards Roma people in Europe before introdu-cing the specific articles in this special issue.

## Racism and everyday bordering

Racism, or, rather, the process of racialization, is a discourse and practice which constructs immutable boundaries between collectivities which is used to naturalize fixed hierarchical power relations between them (Anthias and Yuval-Davis 1992; Goldberg 2009; Rattansi 2007; Solomos and Back 1996).

Barth ([1969] 1998) and others following him have argued that it is the existence of ethnic (and racial) boundaries, rather than of any specific "essence" around which these boundaries are constructed that is crucial in processes of ethnicization and racialization. Any physical or social signifier, from the colour of the skin to the shape of the elbow to accent or mode of dress, can be used to construct the boundaries, which differentiate between "us" and "them". As the different articles in this issue show, although some of the racialization of the Roma can be seen as linked to the white majority's perceptions of Roma as "dark skinned",[3] it is mainly linked traditionally to the anti-nomadism of sedentary populations (see e.g. Kabachnik 2010; McVeigh 1997). However, it is important to emphasize that the racialization of Roma continues also when they become sedentary (as a result of a variety of forced and voluntary social practices and policies) but continue to be, to a large extent, a distinct segment of the labour market. In this way, the Roma case echoes Stuart Hall's famous articulation of "class is the modality in which race is lived" (Hall [1978] 1996).

However, to describe contemporary racialization of Roma only as an intersection of "race" and class is an oversimplification. This racialization is closely linked to particular political projects of belonging (Yuval-Davis 2011) in which Roma are constructed and reconstructed as an "other" by continuous processes of everyday bordering. Different political projects of belonging determine where and according to which criteria the boundaries between the collective self and others would be delineated as well as the permeability and solidity of these boundaries. State borders are but one of the technologies used to construct and maintain these boundaries. It is for this reason that contemporary border studies largely refer to "borderings" rather than to borders; seeing them more as a dynamic, shifting and contested social and political spatial processes rather than just territorial lines (Newman 2006; van Houtum and van Naerssen 2002). However, these borders and boundaries are not just top-down macro social and state policies but are present in everyday discourses and practices (Yuval-Davis, Wemyss, and Cassidy 2017) of different social agents, from state functionaries to the media to all other differentially positioned members of society. All of them are engaged in everyday borderings, however, in somewhat different ways and it is for this reason that we need to add the analytical and methodological perspective of situated intersectionality to our study of everyday bordering (Yuval-Davis 2014).

## Situated intersectionality

Intersectionality (e.g. Anthias 2012; Brah and Phoenix 2004; Crenshaw 1989; Hill Collins 1990; Yuval-Davis 2006) has become a major theoretical and methodological perspective in analysing social relations. Indeed, it is argued that it should be adopted as the most valid approach to analysing social stratification, as it is the most comprehensive, complex and nuanced and does not reduce social hierarchical relations into one axis of power, be it class, race or gender.

The analysis in this special issue follows the specific approach to intersectionality that Yuval-Davis (2014) has named "situated intersectionality". Fundamental to this approach is that intersectionality analysis should be applied to all people and not just to marginalized and racialized women, with whom the rise of Intersectionality theory is historically linked, so as to avoid the risk of exceptionalism and of reifying and essentializing social boundaries.

Epistemologically, intersectionality can be described as a development of feminist standpoint theory, which claims, in somewhat different ways, that it is vital to account for the social positioning of the social agent. Situated gaze, situated knowledge and situated imagination, construct differently the ways we see the world. However, intersectionality theory was interested even more in how the differential situatedness of different social agents relates to the ways they affect and are affected by different social, economic and political projects. In this way it can no doubt be considered as one of the outcomes of the mobilization and proliferation of different identity group struggles for recognition (Taylor 1994). At the same time it can also be seen as a response to some of the problems of identity politics (however important they have been historically in terms of mobilization and exposure of different kinds of oppression), when they conflated social categories and social groupings, individuals and collectives and suppressed the visibility of intra-group power relations and plural voices for the sake of raising the visibility of the social grouping/social category as a whole.

Methodologically, different intersectionality approaches have tended to use what McCall (2005) calls inter- or intra-categorical approaches. By inter-categorical approach McCall means focusing on the way the intersection of different social categories, such as race, gender and class affect particular social behaviour or distribution of resources. Intra-categorical studies, on the other hand, are less occupied with the relationships among various social categories but rather problematize the meanings and boundaries of the categories themselves, such as whether black women were included in the category "women" or what are the shifting boundaries of who is considered to be "black" in particular place and time. Our approach to the study of everyday bordering has seen the two as complementary, combining the sensitivity and dynamism of the intra-categorical approach with the socio-economic perspective of the inter-categorical approach.

Another related issue concerns the importance of differentiating between people's positionings along socio-economic grids of power; their experiential and identificatory perspectives of where they (and others) belong; and their normative value systems (Yuval-Davis 2011, 12–18). These different facets of intersectionality analysis are related to each other but are also irreducible to one other. There is no direct causal relationship between the situatedness of people's gaze and their cognitive, emotional and moral perspectives on life.

Our team has been able to analyse discourses on everyday bordering from differential situated gazes of different social agents in specific locations in several European countries (e.g. politicians, officials, activists, journalists, local residents of different ethnicities both male and female). As can be seen in the articles in this issue which are concerned with media and contesting discourses, we were able to compare intersectional discourses in relation to different temporal points as well as locational.[4]

## Roma in Europe

There are currently between ten and twelve million[5] Roma living in Europe. Estimates are variable, in part, because of the contested nature of Roma identity (Nirenberg 2010). The term Roma was first adopted at the inaugural World Romani Congress in London in 1971. We are aware of the fluid and heterogenous nature of such self-identification, and a number of the papers in the special issue (cf. Wemyss and Cassidy) explore the impacts of homogenizing discourses in more detail. We use the term Roma as the endonym from the Romani language, meaning man, rather than other terms in common usage. Originally from the Indian subcontinent, by the time they were first documented in Europe in the fourteenth century, many were already enslaved and/or excluded and marginalized. Other kingdoms across Europe also put to death, expelled or deported (to colonies in the New World) Roma throughout the sixteenth century when the population spread. Whilst some Roma left Europe for North America from the mid-1800s until the outbreak of the Second World War, these flows were relatively modest. In spite of the genocide of Roma under the Nazi regime, Central and Eastern Europe (CEE) was still home to large numbers of Roma at the end of the Second World War, many of whom were subjected to forced assimilation policies within the newly established state socialist regimes. However, as Ruzicka (2012) has argued, it is important that we do not mask the very different experiences of Roma under state socialism. Under socialism, many Roma were resettled in urban centres in the present-day Czech Republic and these populations were more greatly affected by the "crisis" of transition (Sokol 2001) – deindustrialization leading to high unemployment and the regeneration of inner-city areas, which often displaced them from social housing (Keresztely, Scott, and Virag 2017). Recent academic research and human rights monitors have repeatedly identified a significant decline in the socio-economic status of Eastern European Roma/Gypsies, marked by deepening poverty and increasing levels of residential segregation (Barany 2002; Ladányi and Szelényi 2006).

As a result of multiple national projects of belonging across Europe, which seek to exclude Roma, we have seen the emergence of a frame that posits Roma as a people that exist everywhere but belong nowhere. The enactment of processes of non-belonging in everyday life results in daily practices of seg-regation in schooling, housing, and recreation. These processes of everyday bordering in relation to Roma strengthen the majority population's identity (Fidyk 2013). Roma are effectively banished from the imagined communities of European nations (Anderson 1982). The collapse of state socialism led to emerging Roma engagement with political processes in the fledgling democ-racies, as well as new media and cultural programming in Romani languages. For the Roma, the opening up of channels to the rest of the world presented opportunities for greater international links. However, as Gheorghe (1991) also points out, the removal of state control over the media and other spheres of everyday life in the countries of CEE also led to increases in anti-gypsy dis-courses and even conflict and attacks on Roma people (Puxon 2000). Many of CEE's estimated eight million Roma sought asylum in the West from the mid-1990s. In spite of NGO reports demonstrating institutionalized racism towards the Roma in the Czech Republic and Slovakia their claims were largely refused on the basis that CEE countries were deemed safe, having the required legislative frameworks to protect minority rights (Guy 2003).

Many more Roma live in Europe than are afforded European citizenship, due to systemic processes of exclusion, which make it difficult for them to meet the requirements of "residency-based" citizenship criteria (Guillem 2011). This is not to support the assumption that Roma or Romani culture is inherently or necessarily nomadic, which has often been central to exclusionary processes (Orta 2010; Pusca 2010). The process of EU accession and enlargement has been one of the key reasons for the emergence of a focus on Roma within EU policy circles. The EU has suggested that they and their members have a "special responsibility towards the Roma". Not only are there many more Roma living in the EU since its eastward expansion, but they have also been highly visible in the East–West migration, which has dominated the continent both prior to and following 2004. The extent of the exclusion of the Roma within the Union led the Commission to adopt a Framework to address the complex issues facing Roma people living in all its member states. However, the EU's framing of their approach to addressing Roma exclusion has been highly pro-blematic. First and foremost, because it bolsters national projects of belonging, which exclude Roma by suggesting they are a "European" people. In addition, the EU's usual process of "norm-spreading", which is used to place pressure on member states to conform to particular ideals and values has been strongly resisted by members because of the differing attitudes towards and existing norms relating to Roma.

Although attempts to create a movement focusing on the rights of Roma have been limited by the heterogeneity of the population (McGarry 2012), there are many initiatives being undertaken by Roma activists across Europe. With its roots in the 1920s and 1930s, calls to recognize the Roma as a nation without a state have increased since 1991 and particularly the late 1990s.

Initiatives incorporating Roma into mainstream anti-discrimination policies have largely been perceived as inadequate. It is thanks to the sustained efforts of activists in the heart of the EU's bureaucratic institutions in Brussels and elsewhere that the 2011 European Framework for National Roma Integration Strategies was adopted. Whilst organizations such as the European Roma Rights Centre (ERRC) and European Roma Policy Coalition (ERPC) have broadly welcomed some of the EU's initiatives under the Framework to counter exclusion in the spheres of education, health, housing and employment, a joint statement issued in 2011 expressed their disappointment at the EU's failure to address anti-Gypsyism in member states (ERRC/ERPC 2011). Anti-Gypsyism lies at the heart of Roma exclusion and the EU's Framework can hardly be successful whilst it fails to tackle the associated everyday manifestations of this phenomenon, which include intimidation, harassment and violence against Europe's Roma people. The ERRC continues to advocate for the Framework with partners via the EPRC. In addition, the Centre has also worked on growing its grassroots base by training activists across the region. Some of its programmes also focus on training for professionals, for example, in the legal field, as well as briefings for politicians and policy-makers in Brussels and beyond relating to key themes, such as child protection and gender inequalities.

Whilst the EU's efforts in tackling Roma discrimination should be recognized, there is inevitably the question that in Europeanizing the problems of Roma they risk Europeanizing the solution. This can lead to a homogenizing process, in which realities of local and national contexts and relations disappear. As Vermeersch cautions, "even if problems seem similar, causes may vary a lot from place to place and each community might possess different resources and dynamics to deal with these problems" (2012, 15). Anti-Gypsyism is by no means the same in every country. Roma as a reified ethnic group play different political and social roles within the domestic and international politics of different states.

We sought contributions, which would highlight the multilevel complexities and diversity of Roma experiences of bordering discourses in different and shifting European contexts, that situated dominant and competing discourses about Roma socially and politically and which sought out Roma voices that challenged their representation.

Within the framework of everyday bordering discussed above several themes run through all papers: the recognition of the long histories of discrimination experienced by Roma communities across Europe; the changing policies of the EU and the tension between the inter-European de-bordering and the selective and restrictive immigration policies introduced as each state reacts to free movement in different ways; the continuing racism experienced by Roma people in their interaction with these bordering technologies; the homogenizing "racialized othering" and construction of Roma as a "criminal category" co-existing with the differentiations made between "indigenous" and "migrant" Roma central to the dominant bordering discourses and the heterogeneity, contestations and agency of Roma populations. **The first paper** engages with political and economic issues that contribute to the production of discourses about Roma through focusing on the increased dependency of Romani organizations and media on non-government donors leading to the marginalization of Roma-led advocacy. Plaut explores how the Romani journalism that now dominates aims at intervening to challenge negative representations of Romani populations and at convincing non-Romani populations that Roma can be included in the wider European identity, drowning out Romani activism and advocacy in Roma-targeted media. **The second paper** presents an analysis of how discursive and material processes of urban regeneration in Budapest have contributed to the exclusion of long-standing Roma residents. Keresztély, Scott and Virag expose the political intentions of the local government to marginalize Roma families through re drawing social and spatial borders between social and ethnic groups living in the neighbourhood. **The third paper** extends the analysis beyond the European territorial frame to contrast media discourses in Hungary and Canada about the motivations of and reactions to Hungarian Roma migration to Canada since the 1990s. Varju and Plaut locate the competing discourses in relation to the shifting contexts of the increasingly violent far right politics in Hungary, economic pressures and Canadian migration and welfare policies.

**The fourth paper** explores how Roma from Eastern Europe who have migrated to Finland navigate a "limboscape" where indirect bordering techniques limit their access to social rights and welfare provision. Tervonen and Enache demonstrate that whilst Roma are clear targets of bordering regimes, such regimes are set up to also deal with other legitimate "unwanted migrants". The government's prioritizing of this "hostile environment" has led to inadequate welfare provision whilst migrant Roma employ diverse economic activities and transnational family networks to challenge the effects of such policies.

A similarly "hostile environment" is the context of **the fifth paper** that focuses on the bordering experiences of Roma and non-Roma migrants in the UK. Wemyss and Cassidy track the reproduction and contestation of discourses about EU migration associated with the ending of transitional controls showing that as the restrictions on work by A2 citizens in the UK ended, negative discourses about them conflated diverse Roma and non-Roma groups, extending the border further into the lives of both groups in different and complex ways.

**The final paper** compares how press discourses on the heterogeneous Roma populations of Hungary, Finland and the UK have, since the 1990s, worked as bordering processes differentiating between those who belong to their national collectivities and those who do not. Yuval-Davis, Varju,

Tervonen, Hakim and Fathi relate national level discourses about Roma to the political positions of the press and the politics of governments in the context of EU expansion, securitization and neo-liberal economies. The extent to which the media give space to Roma voices is shown to be influenced by the historical and political contexts of each state. Despite the more recent inclusion of Roma voices, the authors conclusion that the trajectories of the discourses are towards more racialization, criminalization and exclusion and less collective recognition of Roma populations in the three countries resonates with the findings of the other contributors.

## Notes

1. http://www.ohchr.org/EN/Issues/Minorities/SRMinorities/Pages/StudyProtectionRoma.aspx.
2. http://www.euborderscapes.eu/; please also see http://www.uel.ac.uk/cmrb/borderscapes/.
3. Most specifically in the analysis of the "blond Maria" case study in Yuval-Davis et al. (2017).
4. See, for example, Varju and Plaut (2017), Wemyss and Cassidy (2017), and Yuval-Davis et al. (2017).
5. Commission Communication COM/2010/0133 of 7th April on the social and economic integration of the Roma in Europe.

## Acknowledgements

Many thanks to all our partners in the EUBORDERSCAPES research project for their intellectual engagement, in particular we are grateful to those who contributed to work package 9 "Borders, Intersectionality and the Everyday".


## Disclosure statement

No potential conflict of interest was reported by the authors.


## Funding

This work was supported by EUBORDERSCAPES [290775] funded by the European Commission under the Seventh Framework Programme [FP7-SSH-2011-1] Area 4.2.1 The evolving concept of borders.


## References

Acton, T. A. 1997. *Gypsy Politics and Traveller Identity*. Hatfield: University of Hertfordshire Press.

Anderson, B. 1982. *Imagined Communities*. London: Verso.

Anthias, F. 2012. "Hierarchies of Social Location, Class and Intersectionality: Towards a Translocational Frame." *International Sociology* 28 (1): 121–138.

Anthias, F., and N. Yuval-Davis. 1992. *Racialized Boundaries: Race, Nation, Gender, Colour and Class and the Anti-racist Struggle.* Abingdon: Routledge.

Barany, Z. 2002. *The East European Gypsies: Regime Change, Marginality, and Ethnopolitics.* Cambridge: Cambridge University Press.

Barth, F. [1969] 1998. *Ethnic Groups and Boundaries: The Social Organisation of Cultural Difference.* Long Grove, IL: Waveland Press.

Brah, A., and A. Phoenix. 2004. "Ain't I a Woman? Revisiting Intersectionality." *Journal of International Women's Studies* 5 (3): 75–86.

Crenshaw, K. 1989. *Demarginalizing the Intersection of Race and Sex.* Chicago: University of Chicago.

European Roma Rights Centre (ERRC)/European Roma Policy Coalition (ERPC) 2011. "EU Framework Weak on Discrimination Against Roma." April 5. Accessed December 18, 2016. http://www.errc.org/article/eu-framework-weak-on-discrimination-against-roma/3824.

European Roma Rights Centre (ERRC)/European Roma Policy Coalition (ERPC) 2011. "EU Framework Weak on Discrimination Against Roma." April 5. Accessed December 18, 2016. http://www.errc.org/article/eu-framework-weak-on-discrimination-against-roma/3824.

Feys, C. 1997. "Towards a New Paradigm of the Nation: The Case of the Roma." *Journal of Public and International Affairs-Princeton* 8: 1–19.

Fidyk, A. 2013. "Scapegoated in Schools: Reading a Collective Roma Narrative." In *Roma Education in Europe: Practices, Policies and Politics*, edited by M. Miskovic, 42–58. New York: Routledge.

Gheorghe, N. 1991. "Roma-Gypsy Ethnicity in Eastern Europe." *Social Research* 58 (4): 829–844.

Goldberg, D. T. 2009. *The Threat of Race: Reflections on Racial Neoliberalism.* Malden, MA: John Wiley & Sons.

Guillem, S. M. 2011. "European Identity: Across Which Lines? Defining Europe Through Public Discourses on the Roma." *Journal of International and Intercultural Communication* 4 (1): 23–41.

Guy, W. 2003. "'No Soft Touch': Romani Migration to the UK at the Turn of the Twenty-first Century." *Nationalities Papers* 31 (1): 63–79.

Hall, S. [1978] 1996. "Race, Articulation, and Societies Structured in Dominance." In *Black British Cultural Studies: A Reader*, edited by H. A. Baker Jr., M. Diawara and R. H. Lindeborg, 16–60. Chicago: University of Chicago Press.

Hancock, I. F. 2002. *We are the Romani people*, 3446. Hatfield: University of Hertfordshire Press.

Hill Collins, P. 1990. *Black Feminist Thought.* New York: Routledge.

van Houtum, H., and T. van Naerssen. 2002. "Bordering, Ordering and Othering." *Tijdschrift voor economische en sociale geografie* 93 (2): 125–136.

Izsák, R. 2015. "Comprehensive Study of the Human Rights Situation of Roma Worldwide, With a Particular Focus on the Phenomenon of Anti-Gypsyism", Report to the Human Rights Council, June

Kabachnik, P. 2010. "Place Invaders: Constructing the Nomadic Threat in England." *Geographical Review* 100 (1): 90–108.

Keresztely, K., J. W. Scott, and T. Virag. 2017. "Roma Communities, Urban Development and Social Bordering in the Inner City of Budapest." *Ethnic and Racial Studies* 40 (7). doi:10.1080/01419870.2017.1267376.

Klímová-Alexander, I. 2007. "Transnational Romani and Indigenous Non-territorial Self-determination Claims." *Ethnopolitics* 6 (3): 395–416.

Ladányi, J., and I. Szelényi. 2006. *Patterns of Exclusion: Constructing Gypsy Ethnicity and the Making of an Underclass in Transitional Societies of Europe*. New York, NY: Columbia University Press.

Matras, Y. 2002. *Romani: A Linguistic Introduction*. Cambridge: Cambridge University Press.

McCall, L. 2005. "The Complexity of Intersectionality." *Signs: Journal of Women in Culture and Society* 30 (3): 1771–1800.

McGarry, A. 2012. "The Dilemma of the European Union's Roma Policy." *Critical Social Policy* 32 (1): 126–136.

McVeigh, R. 1997. "Theorising Sedentarism: the Roots of Anti-nomadism." In *Gypsy Politics and Traveller Identity*, edited by T. Acton, 7–25. Hatfield: University of Hertfordshire Press.

Newman, D. 2006. "Borders and Bordering towards an Interdisciplinary Dialogue." *European Journal of Social Theory* 9 (2): 171–186.

Nirenberg, J. 2010. "Romani Political Mobilisation from the First International Romani Union Congress to the European Roma, Sinti and Travellers Forum." In *Romani Politics in Contemporary Europe*, edited by N. Sigona and N. Trehan, 94–115. New York: Palgrave Macmillan.

Orta, L. 2010. *Mapping the Invisible: EU-Roma Gypsies*. London: Black Dog.

Pusca, A. 2010. "The 'Roma Problem' in the EU: Nomadism, (In)Visible Architectures and Violence." *Borderlands* 9 (2): 1–17.

Puxon, G. 2000. "The Romani Movement: Rebirth and the First World Romani Congress in Retrospect." In *Scholarship and the Gypsy Struggle*, edited by T. Action, 94–113. Hertfordshire: University of Hertfordshire Press.

Rattansi, A. 2007. *Racism: A Very Short Introduction*. Oxford: Oxford University Press.

Ruzicka, M. 2012. "Continuity or Rupture? Roma/Gypsy Communities in Rural and Urban Environments under Post-socialism." *Journal of Rural Studies* 28 (2): 81–88.

Sokol, M. 2001. "Central and Eastern Europe a Decade after the Fall of State-socialism: Regional Dimensions of Transition Processes." *Regional Studies* 35 (7): 645–655.

Solomos, J., and L. Back. 1996. *Racism and Society*. London: Macmillan.

Taylor, C. 1994. *Multiculturalism*. Edited by A. Gutman. Princeton, NJ: Princeton University Press.

Varjú, V. and S. Plaut. 2017. "Media mirrors? Framing Hungarian Romani Migration to Canada in Hungarian and Canadian Press." *Ethnic and Racial Studies* 40 (7). doi:10.1080/01419870.2017.1266007.

Vermeersch, P. 2012. "Reframing the Roma: EU Initiatives and the Politics of Reinterpretation." *Journal of Ethnic and Migration Studies* 38 (8): 1195–1212.

Wemyss, G., and K. Cassidy. 2017. "'People Think that Romanians and Roma are the Same': Everyday Bordering and the Lifting of Transitional Controls." *Ethnic and Racial Studies* 40 (7). doi:10.1080/01419870.2017.1267381.

Yuval-Davis, N. 2006. "Intersectionality and Feminist Politics." *European Journal of Women's Studies* 13 (3): 193–209.

Yuval-Davis, N. 2011. *The Politics of Belonging: Intersectional Contestations*. London: Sage.

Yuval-Davis, N. 2014. "Situated Intersectionality and Social Inequality." *Raisons Politiques* 58: 91–100.

Yuval-Davis. N., V. Varjú, M. Tervonen, J. Hakim, and M. Fathi. 2017. "Press Discourses on Roma in the UK, Finland and Hungary." *Ethnic and Racial Studies* 40 (7). doi:10.1080/01419870.2017.1267379.

Yuval-Davis, N., G. Wemyss, and K. Cassidy. 2017. *Bordering*. Cambridge: Polity Press.

# Follow the money: international donors, external homelands and their effect on Romani media and advocacy

Shayna Plaut

**ABSTRACT**

While Roma are both Europe's largest minority, there is no "homeland" state that claims to guard their interest. The lack of "an external national homeland" [Brubaker, R. 1996. *Nationalism Reframed: Nationhood and the National Question in the New Europe*. Cambridge: Cambridge University Press] to watchdog and safeguard their rights has a particular effect on how Roma engage as political actors and subjects. International donors/foundations have assumed the role of "external homeland". This article explores the effect that donors' funding priorities have on Romani advocacy – specifically Romani journalism. Drawing upon multi-sited fieldwork in five countries, extensive document analysis, and interviews, I demonstrate that the change in Romani media content over the past two decades reflects the shift in funders' priorities, particularly in relation to the European project. "The Roma" become a tool for donors and European institutions to build a "European" identity while Romani-led advocacy becomes increasingly marganilized.

## Introduction

In 2003, I was invited to Ohrid, Macedonia to observe a meeting of Romani media makers and outlets from across Central and Eastern Europe. For three days, more than thirty people, mostly Roma, engaged in lively discussions of file sharing, video editing, and trans-border news agencies. High hopes were accompanied by ambitious plans. The meeting was jointly organized by Medienhilfe,[1] and the Open Society Foundations (OSF) Network Media Programme.[2] The goal was to create a formal Romani Media Network.

Over a decade later, although there is much more information regarding Roma available via various media outlets, there is still no formal Romani media network. It is unclear whether Medienhilfe is still operational. And, perhaps more importantly, it would be hard today to fill the room with thirty people working specifically in Romani media. This paper focuses on how donors – most notably the OSF and the European Union (EU) – have shifted their priorities regarding Roma over the past decade and how this is reflected in Romani media.[3]

From its origins in the early 1990s Romani media has served two audiences: Romani communities *and* non-Romani populations (ERRC 1999). There was an understanding that if one is to recognize media as both a vehicle and measurement of advocacy, there needed to be support and space for *both* internal conversations *as well as* intervention within dominant discourses. However, since 2005, the targeted population for Romani media is now almost exclusively an international non-Romani audience.

## Terminology and method

This article is based on my fifteen years of scholarly and advocacy work with Romani media throughout Europe, primarily in Central and Eastern Europe. The bulk of the interviews (twenty individuals) referenced were conducted between 2012 and 2014 during multi-sited fieldwork (Hannerz 2003) in London, Budapest, Prague, and Skopje as well as via phone, skype, and email. When information was gathered through interviews (regardless of medium) it is noted as "p.c.". I am deeply grateful to Jeremy Drucker, Tihomir Loza, and Marie Struthers for providing access to documents of their programmes.

In the Romani language "Rom" refers to a Romani man whereas Romni refers to a Romani woman; "Roma" is plural and Romani is both adjectival and the name of the language. A person can be of Romani ethnicity but not consider themselves a "Romani journalist", rather they are a journalist who happens to be Roma. When I use the term "Romani journalism" I refer to media that may, or may not, be made by people who identify as ethnically Romani but rather who hold a Romani positionality (Hill Collins [1986] 2008), that is: media created with a particular Romani lens. Of course, like all people, Roma are heterogeneous and what constitutes a *Romani* frame/lens is not static, nor should it be." (Petrova, Introduction 1999).

## The who, what, where, when, and how of Roma in Europe

As discussed in the introduction to this special issue, there are ten to twelve million Roma estimated to be living across Europe. About eight million Roma reside in former socialist countries, including the former Yugoslavia. The lack of an "external national homeland" as a watchdog state is key because it runs counter to the way national minority rights have traditionally been understood and protected, in law, practice, and politics in Europe (Brubaker 1996), including the right to media in their own language (Downing and Husband 2005; European Convention on the Rights of Minority People, UN Convention on Economic, Social and Cultural Rights). Unlike ethnic Hungarians, Albanians, Serbs, or Germans who reside in other countries, Roma do not have a specific nation-state safeguarding their interests.

Some scholars and activists worry that "Roma" are framed as a people who exist everywhere but belong nowhere: "They (Roma) are thus portrayed as a separate nation without a state" (Vermeersch 2012). Although potentially offering an opportunity to think outside traditional nationalist-driven policy, this is not the case rather, as Vermeersch continues, "By promoting this particular identity frame, however, the Council of Europe unintentionally supports the nationalisms that have pushed the Roma out of the other national communities in Europe" (10). With this logic, Roma do not belong to *all* states, rather they belong to *no* state.

This abdication of home often results in daily practices of segregation in schooling, housing, and recreation. Brubaker explains this process of "dissilimation" policies regarding Jews in many countries in the interwar period with eerie similarities to present-day Roma (1996, 93–96). The relegation of Roma to the margins – physically and in policy – in turn strengthens the majority population's identity (Said [1978] 1994). Roma disappear in urban and rural spaces as well as in discourse and policy. They are simply not considered important enough to be a part of the conversation about the national imaginary (Anderson [1983] 1991; Plaut 2012).

When present in mainstream media, Roma and Romani issues are usually portrayed negatively but most often they are not portrayed at all (Plaut 2012). This may explain the tension surrounding Romani-specific media and media programmes. Although traditional understandings of minority rights recognize the need to have ethnic and linguistically specific media to serve the population's specific needs, some have expressed concerns that doing so exacerbates Romani cultural segregation. This concern has been dismissed by those involved in evaluating such media programmes, pointing out that having a strong Romani cultural identity benefits all domestically and in Europe-wide (Walter 2010).

According to the United Nations and the Council of Europe, Roma are discriminated against in *all* European states. There has been a shift since 2005 to cast Roma as a *European* minority as can be seen in the Decade of Roma Inclusion and most recently in the European Roma Institute and the new Roma Integration 2020 initiative. Again, even when intentions may be good, by Europeanizing the problems of Roma one risks Europeanizing the solution. Thus Roma are reified (by institutions) as a homogenous group; local realities and national contexts are stripped away. This de-contextualization in the name of Europeanization may "leave us with the impression that the situation of the Roma is very similar across Europe and that formula-like solutions can be implemented" (Vermeersch 2012, 15). Although no government in Europe is particularly good to its Romani citizens, the mistreatment and the reasons behind mistreatment are not the same in every country. As Vermeersch cautions, "even if problems seem similar, causes may vary a lot from place to place and each community might possess different resources and dynamics to deal with these problems" (15).

## Roma and the emerging project of democracy: a brief overview

As can be seen in the incongruent EU response to the 2015 "migrant crisis", the political and social concept of "Europe" struggles in policy and politics. In this discord, it has become more difficult to see where the Roma might fit into this discourse of Europe and European-ness. Here is a group of people, living throughout Europe since at least the fourteenth century, suffering from systemic discrimination and, at times, grave human rights abuses, Traditional understandings of European minority politics would suggest that a "kin state" would watchdog their rights, but, there is no "Romanistan".

Perhaps unique to the Romani context, non-state actors – specifically donor organizations, international organizations, and NGOs – have stepped into the traditional role of external homeland with varied levels of success and consistency. Donor organizations, most notably the OSF, have been most active in promoting Romani rights. International organizations such as the World Bank and USAID, some Western European aid agencies and embassies, and some UN agencies have also played an advocacy role. However, the "lobbyists" are external actors with evolving, shifting, and at times competing priorities, even if they have genuine commitment to advocate for Romani rights (Friedman 2014; Sobotka and Vermersch 2012). Funders shift their interests and money, and world affairs or a change of leadership can have a drastic impact on donor priorities.

Although often assumed to be a Central/Eastern European "problem", many Roma have lived for centuries throughout the continent and original EU members do not provide ideal treatment of their own Romani populations. The Copenhagen Criteria[4] were explicit about a candidate country's commitment to minimum standards for the treatment of Roma and other ethnic minorities. However, once countries join the EU there is no incentive to ensure compliance (Bunsecu 2014, 42–43; OSI 2011, 5; Sobotka and Vermersch 2012). Although the EU has increasingly made funds available for Romani issues, it is inconsistent and primarily focused on keeping Roma from accession countries out of Western EU countries. One cannot forget that the EU is a *political* body balancing its internal struggles with the desire to carve out its own identity and agendas as an evolving transnational unit. In fact, according to Bunsescu, in countries such as Romania, Roma were often blamed by politicians and media for delaying accession into the EU (2014, 43, 48–49).

### The danger in "Europeanizing" Roma

The discourse of homogenizing Roma across Europe can quickly slip into "a frame that argues that there is something in the category of "Roma" itself which mandates special treatment" because there is something inherently different about Roma as a group of people (Vermeersch 2012, 10, 14). This becomes especially true in the unfolding project of an expanding Europe, when ideas of what Europe is, and who is European, increase the importance of identity – who is included and excluded. As European identity struggles, it is not difficult to see how conversations about poverty or education change from what can be done to ensure that all members of *our* society enjoy equal rights and protection to "what is it about Roma that causes 'them' to be so different?" This is what Mamdani (2004) calls "Culture Talk".

"Culture Talk" is the idea that there is something inherent in an "other's" culture that explains away socio-economic and political inequalities (Mamdani 2004, Chapter 1). Things like a lack of running water, absence of paved roads, or school segregation – which are the responsibility of the state and greater society – are explained away by "their" culture: "They" are not clean, "They" prefer to live with horses, and "They" do not value school or education. Through a misrepresentation of another's "culture", very real problems, and thus potential solutions, become depoliticized.

The danger of Culture Talk is not only that it is inaccurate, but also that it strips away any agency that "those people" (in this case, Roma) may have in deciding how they want to live; as Mamdani (2004) puts it, "whereas we *have* culture, culture *has* them" (24, my emphasis). Such Culture Talk also serves to strengthen the boundaries between "us" and "them". As Said ([1978] 1994) would offer, by ensuring that Roma are seen as not European, by *not* being Roma, an idea of "European-ness" is strengthened. It also serves to privilege the values, structures, and systems of the non-Roma society as the ideal. Rather than the state addressing the needs of their *citizens* who happen to be Roma, states are now turning to Europe to deal with "their Roma *problem*". This is reinforced through media images of Roma to both Roma and non-Romani audiences.

## The context: history and geography of journalism in Central and Eastern Europe[5]

All states in Central and Eastern Europe have some version of a public broadcasting system recognized as a public service. Since the fall of socialism, media outlets funded partially, if not entirely, by external donors emerged (Mihelj 2011). The diversity and quality of journalism in the region varies considerably and people bemoan the "oligarchy" of the private press; thus public broadcasters become a corrective.[6] However these too are inconsistent. In countries such as the Czech Republic and Romania, public media are considered robust and healthy, whereas the governments of Hungary and Macedonia have been censured by a variety of international organizations for their increased repression of journalists and assault on free speech (Index on Censorship 2013; *Budapost* September 2014).[7] Aside from public media, there is concern in most of the region that much of the private press is tied to the economic and political interests of the owner.[8]

Because the state borders of Europe do not correspond to the linguistic borders of the peoples of Europe, many provisions have been implemented to protect the rights of ethnic and linguistic minorities and to manage potential political strife mobilized in the name of identity (Friedman 1999a, 1999b; Gellner 1983). Protection of national and religious minorities is now presumed to be the state's responsibility (Brubaker 1996; Gellner 1983; Kymlicka 1995). One of these rights is to provide all nations, including minorities, news and entertainment in their own language focusing on issues relevant to their people. This right is upheld both by *not* restricting such media *in addition* to providing financial and bureaucratic assistance, such as printing subsidies, radio/TV frequencies, and/or bandwidth.

If one recognizes that media are a means of both creating and promoting what Barnett and Duvall (2005) refer to as "productive power" – creating political realities through the framing of problems, actors, perpetrators, and possible solutions and thus engaging in agenda setting – then minority media play an interesting role; they both serve a population with information to help with their agenda setting *and* protect this population from encroachment by the majority. Minority media regularly enjoys financial support from the "external homeland" (Brubaker 1996), for example, Hungarian language media in Romania and Slovakia is legally guaranteed by the Romanian and Slovakian state, and financially supported, at least in part, by the Hungarian state.

Minority media are assumed to be in a different language, one that the majority will most likely not understand thus protecting the minority from cultural encroachment by the majority and providing particular information relevant to the community (Downing and Husband 2005; Graham 2010; Lange 2006). This need to protect and develop national and minority cultures has only increased with the enlargement of the EU (Salovaara-Moring 2011; Splichal 2011). If one understands that there is no "god's-eye truth" of media (Zelizer 2004), it is clear that information is selected and presented in cultural and linguistic context and thus promotes that frame. It is also assumed that such media only targets the minority populations. This is not the case for Romani media.

One major difference is that nearly all Roma are fluent in one or more of the dominant languages of the state and thus consume media in that language (Walter 2010; Lange 2006). In addition, with the exception of sporadic funding in Slovenia and Kosovo/a, and minimal but more consistent funding in Macedonia and Slovakia, state governments are *not* supporting Romani media. Rather, funding is coming from international donors.

## Current Romani media landscape in Central/Eastern Europe

The first Romani media can be traced back to Russia in the early 1900s with an increasingly strong presence in Germany after the second World War. Romani journalism became more professionalized in 1970s Yugoslavia and specific Romani programming (rather than translations of state-language broadcasting) is over twenty years old (p.c.: Jankovic). Every country throughout Central and Eastern Europe has, at some point since 1993, been home to a Romani radio and/or TV programme, if not an independent Romani station. In addition, many countries in Northern and Western Europe are home to on-line Romani radio and television stations. However, the quality and consistency of the journalism is very erratic (ERRC 1999; Gross 2006; Lange 2006; Struthers 2008), in part due to erratic project funding which fails to support basic infrastructure, utilities, or salaries.

Most of the media outlets and *all* of the specialized media training and education programmes are the result of external interventions and are not guaranteed consistent funding; thus, they are not an integral part of the larger media landscape. The most consistent funder of these programmes is the network of OSF – primarily the Network Media Programme (the Roma Initiatives Office also has a growing, albeit inconsistent, presence). At its height, (1999–2004) the OSF supported forty-five Romani media outlets through Europe as well as journalism training programmes. Internal assessments done for donors, especially a 2006 report, urged a shift away for Romani media aimed at a Romani audience instead urging a focus on larger, non-Romani populations (Lange 2006; Plaut 2015). When reviewing OSF expenditure sheets there is a dramatic shift in funding priorities within the organization. In an interview in 2013, Lange spoke of the fact that Romani media were not being consumed in the same manner as other minority media noting that because Roma are bi- if not multi-lingual they have a wide range of media options and often chose to watch the better funded and, thus better quality, programming. It is a chicken-and-egg situation: Romani media were not well funded, the quality was often poor, therefore Roma chose to not watch/listen to it regularly and thus more cuts in funding. Although there has been funding for Romani media projects, there has been almost no support granted to individual Romani media *outlets* since the 2006 assessment.

## The role of international funders in framing transnational mobilization

After the fall of state socialism, money, energy, and hope permeated the discourses surrounding Central and Eastern Europe. But many governments, including that of the USA, feared that the overlapping ethnic tapestry of the region could once again be used as a means of dividing people and cause political instability. As the wars of the 1990s showed, these fears were not completely unfounded.

The Organization of Security and Cooperation of Europe (OSCE), the Council of Europe, and the EU engaged many of these countries on a political level. One method was for Western governments, aid organizations, and donor organizations to provide funding to help grow a "civil society" in these new democracies. Civil society was understood to comprise those aspects of society not directly connected to the government including NGOs, cultural and religious organizations, and the media.

Many international funders and policy-makers assumed that, given the similarity of repression across the region, different civil society actors from different countries could learn from each other. Sharing successes and challenges would allow these actors to develop "best practices" leading to cross-border mobilization (Khagram, Riker and Sikkink 2002; Tarrow 2006). Governments would learn to be accountable to their citizenry, citizenry would learn how to hold their governments accountable, and neighbouring countries would hold each other accountable. According to founder and former director of the Network Media Programme, Gordana Jankovic, for those involved in democracy-building, journalism, and journalists are deemed a key component of an open society. The presence or absence of Roma in political and media representation thus reflects much about the larger societies.

## The shift: the Decade of Roma Inclusion 2005–15

By the turn of the twenty-first century, it was evident that there were too many short-term "Roma projects" and not enough coordination (Pusca 2012). Many people, including Roma hired as the translators or coordinators of the projects, joked that a "Roma-industry" was emerging (Nirenberg 2014). As Central and Eastern European countries with large Romani populations were engaged in the process of accession to the EU, it became clear that, unless systemic problems of economic and social exclusion were addressed, Roma were going to migrate to more affluent Western Europe. Many of the governments of Western and Northern Europe saw this as problematic. Thus began a more concerted donor effort at the European level to bring governments of countries with large Romani populations together discussing the role of the state in ensuring Roma "inclusion" in the socio-economic fabric of their countries.

In the Summer of 2003, the Council of Europe Development Bank, the European Commission, the Open Society Institute (OSI), the United Nations Development Programme (UNDP), and the World Bank, as well as the governments of Finland, Hungary, and Sweden sponsored the conference "Roma in an Expanding Europe: Challenges for the Future". In attendance were government representatives from eight countries (Friedman 2014). It is worth noting the unique situation of having NGOs, Inter-Governmental Organizations, and state governments focused on both national and transnational goals.

It was at this meeting that the 2005–15 Decade of Roma Inclusion ("The Decade") was announced. The Decade was an initiative that aimed to coordinate state initiatives and attention about Roma that had previously been handled by a variety of overlapping NGO projects.[9] Four priorities of inclusion were established: education, employment, housing, and health care, all of which, according to international and domestic law, are understood as responsibilities of the state. There were also two cross-cutting themes: gender mainstreaming and discrimination. While the focus and structure of The Decade was still being negotiated, there was an effort to include media and discrimination as formal foci but neither was included. As Gordana Jankovic explained, "The Decade was a lost opportunity for strengthening further the Romani media – but there were other very important issues on the agenda and The Decade could not address everything" (p.c.).

This has occurred in tandem with the larger policy shift from "addressing" Romani issues within a human rights frame (a context-specific denouncement of the violation, strategy, and mobilization) to "including" Roma within the state and the larger European project (Sobotka and Vermersch 2012; p.c.: Petrovski). Many have identified this "lost opportunity" as the beginning of a shift in the goals and priorities of Romani media. Rather than serving the interests and needs of Romani populations, Romani media have become a method to reach state and European audiences (p.c.: Jovanović, Moricz, and Skopljanac).

### Direct impact on media content and framing

Although there are some independent projects such as online television shows and radio stations run out of people's bedrooms, there is no longer *any* systemic financial or institutional support to create media specifically crafted for Romani people.[10] I argue this not only reflects, but shapes, the larger approaches to Romani advocacy. Before, Romani media, often in a mix of Romani and the state language(s), would serve as a forum for the Roma community in terms of news, concerns, entertainment, resources, and announcements of important social happenings locally, nationally, regionally, and globally – what Gitlin (1998) refers to as a "mini-spherical". Although the information was at times benign, even seemingly trivial (song dedications for weddings, births, and circumcisions were particularly prevalent in the Balkans) it served an important role in community cohesion (ERRC 1999; Gross 2006; Lange 2006). In addition, both radio and television required state cooperation to secure telecommunications frequency thus ensuring at least a minimum of *state* buy-in. Now, with very rare exceptions, in order to secure donor funding, there is a mandate for *inter-state* cooperation (p.c.: Loza and Dekic). This has led to an increase in the technical quality of the product but it has also led to a significant change in content.

According to Marie Struthers, former senior programme director for NMP who oversaw the Romani media portfolio, increasingly, Romani media has turned into "good-quality Romani content" (p.c.). The effect was often using media content and process to "showcase Roma and Romani issues" to non-Romani audiences. This can be seen most notably in the 2014 five-story compilation *Europe: Homeland for the Roma* which received EU and OSF funding. The project, like almost all projects now, had teams of Romani and non-Romani journalists working together in five EU countries with high Romani populations: Czech Republic, Slovakia, Hungary, Romania, and Bulgaria. International trainers from North America were brought into work with the teams to produce highly polished feature shorts.

It is beautifully shot and the website is highly polished however there is no clear audience. When asked about audience, the lead trainers and organizers, kept saying "everyone" (p.c.: Beckman and Loza). Although on the surface this can appear positive (the bigger, the better, the more impact!), I argue that such a move is quite dangerous: by targeting "everyone" very real and nuanced economic, political, and social problems as well as potential solutions are co-opted by a larger European talk of "tolerance".

## Journalists' and donor's perspectives on journalism

Professional journalists often do a delicate dance of providing accurate and critical information without wanting to be perceived as the framers of the issues themselves – as this could cross into advocacy (El Naway and Iskander 2002; Plaut 2014, 2015; Zelizer 2004). Being seen as an advocate would thus decrease a journalist's credibility as a journalist (Wade 2011). Journalists can help move issues up the ladder of media importance, but they do not want to be seen as writing the agenda.

However, drawing such a clear distinction between informing a citizenry and advocacy was not always a priority for the donors. The OSF's Network Media Programme began funding media outlets in the 1980s, even before the fall of state socialism. When I asked Jankovic specifically *how* Romani journalism helped serve the larger goals of the OSF, she was puzzled by the question:

> Well, OSF sees itself as building a vibrant and tolerant society to empower and promote democracy for all communities in all spaces. The Romani community is one of the largest communities in Europe. You can't marginalize a large community in these societies and then claim that you have an open society. (p.c.)

Jankovic's assessment of the connection between a "vibrant and tolerant society" that "empower[s] and promotes democracy" and journalism is based on assumptions about the role of the media. In her view, the media's role goes beyond strictly reporting; rather, media should be informing and educating the public , not just reflecting society but formulating the issues that are, or should be, of concern within society (Barnett and Duvall 2005; Fairclough 1992, 1995; Hallin 1994). My (SP) interview with Jankovic continued:

GJ: Media helps formulate the issues; it helps to contextualize the issues for both minority and majority communities and helps build a debate. It helps in building democracies.

SP: That is a very specific role for media – how does this work with the larger ideas and guiding principles of objectivity, unbiased, credibility ... ?

GJ: Independent journalism has all those characteristics. Those don't go away. There is a need for the additional function – a need to have a mission for the society you serve. Media are reflecting political discussion of the country and of particular groups, for example, ethnic groups, but in doing so journalism can still maintain independence and non-partisan approaches (p.c.)

It is interesting to note that this process of reflecting and formulating issues for majority and minority societies is still done within the framework of good, independent (non-partisan) journalism. This is clear in Jankovic's words: "Independent journalism has all those characteristics. Those don't go away".[11]

Because the goal of Romani journalism has changed from covering Romani issues for a Romani audience to producing "good-quality Romani content" for a mainstream audience (p.c.: Struthers), the language used to describe the field has changed. Struthers explained that, rather than "Romani media" or "Romani journalists", the preferred term is now "Romani media initiatives". This broader term includes filmmaking, news agencies, blogging, or "whatever it is that furthers good-quality content on Roma issues and is able to reach and speak with credibility to *as large an audience as possible*" (p.c.: Struthers, my emphasis). Struthers pointed out that this work can be done by Romani or non-Romani media makers and broadcast on Romani or non-Romani media outlets.

Although there is an increasing interest by funders in creating regional media programmes and partnerships (three or more countries), many of the Romani journalists and journalism trainers point to the need to intervene in the increasingly racist and incendiary local media (Sobotka and Vermersch 2012). Examples include the coverage of the now-infamous wall dividing the Roma and non-Roma neighbourhoods of Usti nad Labem in the Czech

Republic and segregated schooling in Hungary and Bulgaria. Whereas the national media were often critical, the local press fanned the flame of racism. Those involved in running the journalism programmes recognize the specificity of the socio-political, economic, and cultural context and how it affects Roma and non-Roma populations. As evidenced by Sosinet.hu and Tocak, two online news sources funded primarily by OSF and run by domestic NGOs, there is a slow move towards producing more media in local languages for domestic press and local language news sites. Although these local media productions are well trafficked by local and national media – at times breaking stories – when reviewing expenditure sheets it is evident that funding is minimal and inconsistent which also reflects the quality of the journalism and journalism training (p.c.: Cox, Dervišbegović and Loza).

## From media outlets to media projects

My findings indicate that this shift in the goals for Romani media is reflective of changing, and strategic approaches to Romani people and issues at state, regional, and European levels. This can be seen in the EU mandating multi-state cooperation for nearly all of their Romani journalism projects. Overwhelmingly, Romani journalism is dependent on funding from donors whose goal is to bring about socio-political change. In fact, as noted earlier, Lange's 2006 report commissioned by the OSF Network Media Programme was both instrumental and symptomatic. It was symptomatic that the OSF felt a need to re-evaluate what constituted "successful" Romani media programmes and content in the context of the Decade of Roma Inclusion. It was instrumental in that its findings justified the shift in the OSF's understanding and financial support of Romani media initiatives. Thus, the change in journalism is reflected in the changes in politics and vice versa.

Donors, grantees, and external assessors all agree that the funding provided to Romani media and media programmes have been "insufficient or inefficient" (Gross and Spaskovska 2011; Lange 2006; Struthers 2008, 59). Both Struthers and Jankovic were uncomfortable with some of the changes they oversaw in the Network Media Programme for Romani media, noting that long-term financial commitment to journalism education and institutional support to outlets is necessary but no longer available. (p.c.: Jankovic, Struthers, Struthers 2008, 63).

Whereas many other minority media are supported at least in part through public funds, Romani media are surviving on project-based funding severely affecting the range and quality of the content they can deliver and expectations for the future (Struthers 2008, 59). One effect of this project-based donor dependence is that Romani journalists must perform many, at times contradictory, roles. Those working at Romani media outlets have to be journalists, marketing managers, and technicians, and moreover must become experts at looking for grants and applying for funds (p.c.: Rethy, and Jovanović). Many people with whom I spoke referred to the process as "begging", OSF. Željko Jovanović, the current director of the OSF's Romani Initiatives Programme, jokingly reflected on his experience as a former director of a Romani radio station in Serbia that depended on OSF funds: "We became OSF junkies" (p.c.). In other words, when the donors go, the money goes, and the media outlet itself goes into withdrawal and folds. This is opposed to a publically funded model of journalism that recognizes and supports journalism, as part of a larger public good *not* a money making venture (Strömbäck 2005).

Everyone I interviewed recognized that the current donor model is not sustainable and certainly not desirable, lamenting: "It is the way it is" (p.c.: Dekic, Druker, and Loza).[12] Professional journalists expressed the particular concern that media were run in an "NGO culture" (p.c.: Dekic and Dervišbegović), noting the quality and depth of the journalism were directly connected to the amount of funds available at the time. When I asked people if they felt frustrated, they sighed almost in resignation. As Slobodanka Dekic, Project Coordinator for Media Centar Sarajevo, explained:

> It's not frustration; it's reality. It is something that happened to most of these kinds of media in the region. Because everything was really project driven, nothing came from inside. So in the beginning you have to deal with what will happen once the funds stop.

This lack of sustainability is disheartening for all NGO projects, but for media, built and surviving on reputation, it is particularly damaging. How does one establish their "brand" as a trusted media outlet (p.c.: Struthers) when they may disappear in a year or two? The response from many of the directors of journalism programmes and media centres was that it was impossible, but, for the sake of the larger society, they needed to try. This is captured below from my (SP) interview with Dekic (SD):

SD:   … the funders and international organizations somehow expect to achieve sustainability, which is really ridiculous because this kind of content will never achieve sustainability.
SP:   So then why do you keep doing it?
SD:   Still working with journalism?
SP:   Still working with journalism … still working with journalists …
SD:   Why not? I mean, it's like asking, "Why you eat today if you are going to be hungry tomorrow?"

## Roma as the canary in the (European) coalmine

Former Czech president and playwright Vaclav Havel famously said the treatment of Roma becomes the "litmus test" for the health of a free society (as cited in Kamm, 1993). In a similar spirit, I repeatedly heard from journalists that the treatment of Roma can be understood as the "canary in the coalmine" in terms of how other citizens in Europe can, or will, be (mis)treated in the future (p.c.: Moricz, Saracini, field notes, 22 May 2013).

Many of the other journalists and coordinators of journalism training who were originally from Europe spoke of the treatment of Roma as "an embarrassment" to Europe and to the idea of Europe as a union of democracies. Tihomir Loza, a journalist and journalism trainer who has lived and worked in both the Balkans and the UK, was clear when he referred to the treatment of Roma as one of – if not the – greatest current human rights abuses in Europe (p.c.). All those involved in covering Romani issues – journalists, trainers, coordinators, and funders – assumed that notions of liberal democracy could be put in motion by using journalism to inform and educate; that calling attention to Romani issues through media has the potential to galvanize the citizenry to pressure their societies and governments into action (p.c.: Dekic, Jordan, and Moricz).

In short, donors, trainers, and journalists alike see stories about how Roma are treated and mistreated, as well as empowering stories about Roma as strengthening the democratic project. This approach to "bridging" Romani and non-Romani society is assumed to help fold Roma into the citizenry of dominant society. The goal for donors and journalism trainers appears to be "Europeanization": to counteract racism and intolerance in the name of European values. In this way the state and the dominant culture within the state are still held as the norm, and media covering Roma become a kind of intervention.

## Concluding discussion and possible ways forward

From the mid-1990s through the mid-2000s, the OSF invested in Romani media outlets and Romani training programmes. The goal was to create Romani media based on the minority media model common throughout Europe but without the political will and pressure often exercised by an "external homeland" (Brubaker 1996; Gross and Spaskovska 2011). Most of the training programmes were evaluated as successes, but the Romani media outlets themselves were not (Lange 2006). Now, a cadre of increasingly highly skilled Romani journalists (and non-Romani journalists with a particular interest in Romani issues) exists, but funding for the stories has been drying up. Journalism as a field is struggling, and journalism within Central and Eastern Europe is facing the competing pressures of increased politicization, media restrictions, and capitalism run amok. Journalists are losing their jobs, and a journalist without a place to run his or her work is not a working journalist.

From grant applications written since 2009, it is evident that a new trend is emerging: media platforms *are* built into the training programme schemes (Transitions 2009, 2010). This enables the participants to have an outlet and develop a portfolio while also exposing the content to a real audience. In addition, because of EU funds and the push towards more online journalism, since 2005 programmes have become increasingly transnational both in terms of content and participants. However, as noted above, the outlets are not financially self-sustaining, and neither the states nor the EU have the political will to ensure sustained journalism and journalistic outlets. Both journalists and editors must be paid.

Everyone I interviewed, including the funders, believed that media focusing on human rights, minority issues, and Romani issues were an essential part of a healthy, democratic society and yet were never going to be profitable in the marketplace. Most believed that Romani media should be supported by public funds, but, if they were not, that donors and funders needed to step in without stigma and strangling regulations (p.c.: Jovanović, Loza, and Moricz). According to Ilona Moricz, the director of the Centre for Independent Journalism mainstream journalists often avoid covering certain issues, "especially in difficult political times", which must be "corrected" by what she and others refer to as "non-profit journalism". Moricz added that she believes non-profit journalism "will never be sustainable. Community media or minority media will never be sustainable. It is a myth ... but it serves the interest of the public and therefore must exist" (p.c.). Everyone interviewed agreed that this kind of media needs to be in the public sphere as a kind of "public service" to *all* of society.

Donors and journalists believe that in order to have a healthy, democratic society, a vibrant media must address, reflect, and formulate issues important to the growth of the society. This media needs to include, or perhaps must especially include, those who are often marginalized, as such perspectives can often more accurately show the machinations of power in the entire society (Harding 1993). The strategy amongst donors to Romani media that has gained the most prestige at this time is to have Romani voices, perspectives, and realities seen and recognized *as equals* by the non-Romani population. Non-Roma embody the standard in which progress is measured and thus power is still assumed to be defined by, and thus reside with, the non-Romani populations.

In short, the "Europeanization" of Romani issues by donors/foundations, state governments, and the EU shifts the conversation from speaking to – and with – Roma to that of inclusion. I argue that this approach strengthens a liberal form of multicultural democracy and citizenship yet co-opts potential Romani-led change. Romani media projects are increasingly focused on convincing the larger non-Romani population that Roma too are citizens and part of European society. Rarely is anyone questioning what society Roma are being included into and, what in the process, is being left out.

Racism against Roma throughout Europe is rising and socio-economic conditions for Roma are getting worse, however the tensions of power are not only between Roma and non-Romani segments of society but rather: rural

26

and urban, governmental accountability, decentralization, and the promises of the EU. By framing the problem and solution in terms of "tolerance" the realities of politics becomes obscured – shifting the conversation once again to culture and away from power. Large multi-state projects of "Romani content" can often inadvertently perpetuate Culture Talk and strip Roma of their agency leaving them as simply victims begging for inclusion. This is even more dangerous when there are no longer smaller, Romani media, to provide a space for discussion, dissent and alternatives.[13] I am arguing that this *lack* of consistent funding is evidence of the states failing in their responsibilities to their citizens. As with other ethnic minorities, states must provide the financial and structural support for Romani media outlets catering to Romani populations within that country or smaller municipalities. In addition, there is a need to target the larger, non-Romani populations living in the state in order to intervene in the dominant discourse. Lastly, European-wide media projects can help serve to better educate Roma and non-Roma about one another, particularly as a means to counteract the overwhelmingly negative media coverage in the post-Schengen era of high unemployment and visa-free travel.

## Notes

1. A Swiss NGO under the direction of Nena Skopljanac, originally from Bosnia.
2. In 2014, the Network Media Programme changed its name to the Independent Journalism Programme.
3. I am not Roma, nor did I grow up in Europe. I *do* speak, read and write the Arli dialect of Romani.
4. The standards originally drafted in 1993 for all new accession countries seeking entry into the EU.
5. This section heading is inspired by Salovaara-Moring's (2011) work. I use the term "'Central and Eastern Europe" to include all former socialist countries in Europe, including those of the former Yugoslavia.
6. Repression in Hungary and Macedonia has increased markedly since 2010 – from strategic audits and libel cases to requiring journalists to register with the government, imprisonment and disappearances. According to the Center for Independent Journalism, there is no longer independent press in Hungary (p.c.: Moricz). In 2009 under a new media law, Macedonia slipped from 34th to 116th out of 179 countries in terms of media freedom (*Balkan Media Watch* 2013, OSCE).
7. http://www.whitehouse.gov/the-press-office/2014/09/23/remarks-president-clinton-global-initiative and most recently, the 2014 Press Freedom Report https://euobserver.com/news/127604.
8. p.c.: Loza, Dervišbegović, Moricz.
9. The Decade of Roma Inclusion (2005–2015) was a joint initiative established by the World Bank and OSF. Member countries were obligated to draft national action plans intended to become part of their national legislation and initiatives. The Decade did not have an external budget rather member states pool funds. In 2015, a new initiative, Roma Integration 2020 was launched by the CoE and OSF.

10. Many of these online media outlets are located in Western Europe but founded by people originally from former Yugoslavia.
11. Although it is beyond the scope of this paper, it is interesting to note that "good journalism" is understood as journalism that meets "Western professional standards" – specifically, diversity of sources, credibility, fact checking, and transparency – within the Anglo-American tradition (p.c.: Struthers).
12. Loza explained there is an undeserved "stigma" to donor-supported media. This journalism, often referred to as "public service journalism" or "non-profit journalism" is non-partisan and non-commercial often employing feature writing and in-depth investigative reporting which are more time and labour intensive. What Loza and others note is that such stigma does not extend to the publically supported BBC or other, well-respected, public media (p.c.).
13. Numerous critical scholars have spoken about the need for communities that are removed from spheres of formal political power. This enables a space for communication and debate enabling nuance and claim-making (Fraser 1991; Downing and Husband 2005).

## Acknowledgements

This paper is over a decade in the making. Thanks to Yana Gorokhovskiai and Carla Winston for their patient and extensive feedback. Versions were presented at "Eurasian States and Societies: Past and Present" at Green College at UBC (2014), the Association for the Study of Nationalities (2015) and "Beyond Gypsy Stereotypes: Voicing Romani Pluralities" (2015). I thank all in attendance for their questions and especially Lisa Sundstrom, Alexy Golubev, Alexia Bloch, and Carol Silverman. I am always grateful to Eben Friedman's keen eye and critical insights.

## Disclosure statement

No potential conflict of interest was reported by the author.

## Funding

This work was supported by The Government of Canada's Social Science and Humanities Council, Vanier Fellowship.

## References

Anderson, B. (1983) 1991. *Imagined Communities: Reflections on the Origin and Spread of Nationalism*. London: Verso.
Barnett, M., and R. Duvall. 2005. "Power in Global Governance." In *Power in Global Governance*, edited by M. Barnett and R. Duvall, 1–32. Cambridge: Cambridge University Press.
Brubaker, R. 1996. *Nationalism Reframed: Nationhood and the National Question in the New Europe*. Cambridge: Cambridge University Press.
Bunsecu, I. 2014. *Roma in Europe. The Politics of Collective Identity Formation*. London: Ashgate.
Downing, J., and C. Husband. 2005. *Representing Race: Racisms, Ethnicity and the Media*. London: Sage.

El-Nawawy, M., and A. Iskandar. 2002. "The Minotaur of 'Contextual Objectivity': War Coverage and the Pursuit of Accuracy with Appeal." *Transnational Broadcasting Studies* 9. http://www.tbsjournal.com/Archives/Fall02/Iskandar.html.

ERRC. 1999. Romani Media/Mainstream Media, Romani Rights, 4. http://www.errc.org/roma-rights-journal/roma-rights-4-1999-romani-mediamainstream-media/1134.

Fairclough, N. 1992. *Discourse and Social Change*. Cambridge: Polity Press.

Fairclough, N. 1995. *Media Discourse*. London: Edward Arnold.

Fraser, N. 1991. "Rethinking the Public Sphere: A Contribution to the Critique of Actually Existing Democracy." In *Habermas and the Public Sphere*, edited by C. Calhoun, 109–142. Cambridge, MA: MIT Press.

Friedman, V. 1999a. "Observing the Observers: Language, Ethnicity, and Power in the 1994 Macedonian Census and Beyond." In *Toward Comprehensive Peace in Southeastern Europe: Conflict Prevention in the South Balkans*, edited by B. Rubin, 81–105. New York: Council on Foreign Relations/Twentieth Century Fund.

Friedman, V. 1999b. "The Romani Language in the Republic of Macedonia: Status, Usage, and Sociolinguistic Perspectives." *Acta Linguistica Hungarica* 46 (3–4): 317–339.

Friedman, E. 2014. *Decade of Roma Inclusion Progress Report*. Bratislava: United Nations Development Programme.

Gellner, E. 1983. *Nations and Nationalism*. Ithaca, NY: Cornell University Press.

Gitlin, T. 1998. "Public Sphere or Public Sphericules?'." In *Media, Ritual, Identity*, edited by T. Liebes, and J. Curran, 168–175. London: Routledge.

Graham, L. M. 2010. "A Right to Media?" *Columbia Human Rights Law Review* 41: 429–507.

Gross, P. 2006. "A Prolegomena to the Study of the Romani Media in Eastern Europe." *European Journal of Communication* 21: 477–497.

Gross, P., and K. Spaskovska. 2011. "Aiding Integration and Identity: The Unfulfilled Roles and Functions of the Romani Media in Eastern Europe." In *Media, Nationalism and European Identities*, edited by M. Sokosd and K. Jakubowicz, 153–170. Budapest: CEU Press.

Hallin, D. 1994. *We keep America on Top of the World: Television Journalism and the Public Sphere*. New York, NY: Routledge.

Hannerz, U. 2003. "Being There … and There … and There! Reflections on Multi-site Ethnography." *Ethnography* 4 (2): 201–216. doi:10.1177/14661381030042003.

Harding, S. 1993. "Rethinking Standpoint Epistemology: What Is 'Strong Objectivity?'." In *Feminist Epistemologies*, edited by L. Alcoff and E. Potter, 49–82. New York: Routledge.

Hill Collins, P. (1986) 2008. "Learning from the Outsider within: The Sociological Significance of Black Feminist Thought." In *Just Methods: An Interdisciplinary Feminist Reader*, edited by A. Jaggar, 308–320. Boulder, CO: Paradigm.

Kamm, H. 1993. "Havel Calls the Gypsies 'Litmus Test.'" *The New York Times,* December 10. Accessed May 16, 2014. http://www.nytimes.com/1993/12/10/world/havel-calls-the-gypsies-litmus-test.html.

Khagram, S., J. V. Riker, and K. Sikkink. 2002. *Restructuring World Politics: Transnational Social Movements, Networks, and Norms*. Minneapolis: Minnesota University Press.

Kymlicka, W. 1995. *Multicultural Citizenship*. Oxford: Oxford University Press.

Lange, Y. 2006. *Roma (in the) Media* [Review Commissioned by the Open Society Foundations]. Copy in possession of author.

Mamdani, M. 2004. *Good Muslim, Bad Muslim*. New York: Three Leaves Press.

Mihelj, S. 2011. *Media Nations: Communication Belonging and Exclusion in the Modern World*. London: Palgrave MacMillian.

Nirenberg, J. 2014. *Gypsy Movements*. Tampa: Schlimmer Publishing.

OSI (Open Society Institute). 2011. *Beyond Rhetoric: Roma Integration Roadmap for 2020*. Budapest, Hungary: Createch.

Petrova, D. 1999. "Competing Romani Identities [Special Issue]." *Roma Rights Introduction*, no. 3. http://www.errc.org/cikk.php?cikk=965.

Plaut, S. 2012. "Expelling the Victim by Demanding Voice: The Counterframing of Transnational Romani Activism." *Alternatives: Global, Local, Political* 37 (1): 52–65.

Plaut, S. 2014 "'Fact Based Storytelling' or Fact Based Activism? Tensions, Strategies and Next Steps of Human Rights and Journalism." In *Sage Handbook of Human Rights*, edited by A. Mijhr, and M. Gibney. Thousand Oaks, CA: Sage.

Plaut, S. 2015. "'Reshaping the Borders of Journalism: Lessons Learned from Transnational Peoples' Journalism." *Journalism Practice*. 1–32. doi:10.1080/17512786.2015.1092391.

Pusca, A. 2012. *Eastern European Roma in the EU: Mobility, Discrimination, Solutions*. International Debate Education Associates. New York: Idebate Press.

Said, E. [1978] 1994. *Orientalism*. New York, NY: Vintage Press.

Salovaara-Moring, I. 2011. "What is Europe? Geographies of Journalism." In *Media, Nationalism and European Identities*, edited by M. Sokosd and K. Jakubowicz, 49–71. Budapest: CEU Press.

Sobotka, E., and P. Vermersch. 2012. "Governing Human Rights and Roma Inclusion: Can the EU be a Catalyst for Local Social Change?" *Human Rights Quarterly* 34: 800–822.

Splichal, S. 2011. "Transnationalization/Europeanization of the Public Sphere/s." In *Media, Nationalism and European Identities*, edited by M. Sokosd and K. Jakubowicz, 21–47. Budapest: CEU Press.

Strömbäck, J. 2005. "In Search of a Standard: Four Models of Democracy and Their Normative Implications for Journalism." *Journalism Studies* 6 (3): 331–345.

Struthers, M. 2008. "Strategic Support of Roma Media Initiatives. Media on the Move: Migrants and Minorities and the Media." Proceedings of the fourth Symposium Forum Media and Development (FoME), Bonn, Germany. Accessed March 22, 2013. http://www.cameco.org/files/mediaonthemove-struthers.pdf.

Tarrow, S. (2006). *The New Transnational Activism*. New York, NY: Cambridge Press.

Transitions. 2009. *EuropeAid Grant Application: Advancing Roma Visibility, a Project Aimed at Improving Media Reporting of Roma Communities in the Balkans* [Grant application]. Copy in possession of author.

Transitions. 2010. *Proposal for Continuation of 'Romani Journalist Advancement Project'* [Grant Application]. Copy in possession of author.

Vermeersch, P. 2012. "Reframing the Roma: EU Initiatives and the Politics of Reinterpretation." *Journal of Ethnic and Migration Studies* 38 (8), 1195–1212. doi:10.1080/1369183X.2012.689175.

Wade, L. 2011. "Journalism, Advocacy and the Social Construction of Consensus." *Media, Culture & Society* 33: 1166–1184. doi:10.1177/0163443711418273.

Walter, M. 2010. *Review of Transitions Roma and Education Programs* [Review commissioned by the Open Society Foundations.] Copy in possession of author.

Zelizer, B. 2004. "When Facts, Truth and Reality are God-terms: On Journalism's Uneasy Place in Cultural Studies." *Communication and Critical/Cultural Studies* 1 (1), 100–119. doi:10.1080/147914204200018095.

# Roma communities, urban development and social bordering in the inner city of Budapest

Krisztina Keresztély, James W. Scott and Tünde Virág

**ABSTRACT**

The paper relates intersectionality to the construction of urban borders based on a case study of Roma neighbourhoods in Budapest. In doing this the authors focus on rationales behind appropriating and demarcating urban spaces according to political, ethno-territorial and economic agendas. We are concerned with bordering as reflected in representations of neighbourhood in Budapest's VIII District and socio-ethnic issues that have been framed in conjunction with urban development. This includes the selective ways Roma-specific issues are made visible, or in fact masked, through ostensibly "colour-blind" policies. Furthermore, we relate these representations to concrete impacts of urban renewal with regard to challenges of multi-ethnicity but also to often exclusionary practices of border-making. Indeed, while not an officially proclaimed policy, social segregation is eagerly pursued in practice. However, this is only part of the story as we can clearly identify attempts to create a sense of Roma belonging and pride.

## Introduction

The "bordering" concept now in wide academic use suggests that the making of borders is a highly political and reflexive process, both as a formal and a socio-cultural exercise of power and authority, but also as a very basic social practice in terms of the construction of sense of identity and place (Scott 2012). van Houtum, Kramsch, and Zierhofer (2005) refer to everyday "bordering and ordering" practices that create and recreate new social-cultural boundaries and divisions which are also spatial in nature. Everyday lived experiences include intersections, differentiations and similarities. As Rhodes (2012) has argued, cognitive boundary-making can also contribute to geographies of difference through the stigmatization of specific places – places where danger, deviance and degradation are to be found.

Consequently, borders are essential to place-making while place-making is itself about the appropriations of space by different actors and for different purposes. Here, we investigate processes of everyday bordering as a form of place-making and how they both involve and impact Roma communities of inner-city Budapest. At one level we investigate the reimaging of an inner-city neighbourhood of Budapest through policies of urban development and regeneration as well as through bottom-up appropriations of neighbourhood spaces. At the same time, we are equally interested in the impacts of these place-making exercises which are informed not only by explicit economic and design agendas but also by implicit socio-ethnic objectives. The local Roma population is particularly vulnerable to the vicissitudes of urban renewal and we will hence consider links between socio-cultural borderings of urban spaces and the top-down, often punitive regulation of access to those spaces.

The specific case that will be developed here involves a traditionally multiethnic and multicultural area of Budapest, the VIII District or Józsefváros. Within this larger administrative area, our study reconstructs developments in the Magdolna neighbourhood which during the early 2000s became the focus of Budapest's – and East-Central Europe's – first socially integrative urban renewal programme. Urban redevelopment is of course not simply a policy; in addition to its economic rationalities, political motivations and physical impacts it has concrete socio-spatial consequences for neighbourhoods and specific groups. Recreating place image and identity can and does often involve the sorting out of groups that disturb or do not conform to a politically desired sense of well-organized neighbourhoods and public spaces. And yet, the situation is generally more complex than a simple narrative of middle-class "revanchism" (Smith 1996) in which the rich retake inner cities from the poor and homeless. Neighbourhoods are seldom surfaces that are wiped clean of their pasts and place identities by gentrification. Furthermore, the process of re-appropriating neighbourhood spaces is often about socio-ethnic and cultural "re-borderings" and not simply, to paraphrase Mitchell (2003) the crossing of "neo-liberal lines".

This case study will develop bordering perspectives that shed light on the rationales behind appropriating and demarcating social spaces within cities as means to promote political, ethno-territorial and economic agendas. Clearly, bordering does not take place in a cognitive vacuum but reflects a constant interaction with social, political and economic environments and concrete physical spaces. In following the general approach outlined by Yuval-Davis (2011, 2015), namely that of situated intersectionality and everyday bordering, our methodology indicates how different appropriations and representations of neighbourhood spaces reflect the social positionality of social actors. We therefore assume that politics of place-making and belonging – and not exclusively socio-economic processes such as gentrification – are conditioning neighbourhood change in post-socialist Budapest; they reflect agency, for example, in specific choices regarding housing, public spaces and other uses of public funds. In terms of the information gathered, we have addressed three specific issues: (1) the general situation, policies and actions regarding the exclusion/cohesion of the Roma minority in Hungary and in Budapest, (2) the specific situation of the VIII District of Budapest and its social urban regeneration policies and (3) the general social, spatial and political consequences of bordering processes.

In reflecting the main insights of our research, we develop two major analytical perspectives. With the first we are concerned with bordering as reflected in representations of neighbourhood in the VIII District and socio-ethnic issues that have been framed in conjunction with urban development issues. This includes the selective ways Roma-specific issues are made visible, or in fact masked, through ostensibly "colour-blind" policies. Secondly, we will relate these representations to the concrete impacts of local urban renewal policies with regard to challenges of multi-ethnicity but also to often exclusionary practices of border-making. As we will indicate in our discussion, social segregation is not an official policy but is eagerly pursued in practice. However, this is only part of the story as we can clearly identify attempts to create a sense of Roma belonging and pride.

Our case study is not intended to be representative of the totality of Roma communities in Hungary. While Józsefváros' experience is not unique in terms of marginalization it is, nevertheless, quite distinct in terms of the strategies, trajectories and social impacts of urban development. Following Yin (2003) we adhere to the notion that one important purpose of singular case studies is to speak to a specific theoretical and conceptual argument in ways that have not been widely developed. We take up a single case design in order to develop an approach that, among others, links public policies, bordering processes and Roma marginalization. Our work indicates that the visible effects of urban regeneration programmes in the Magdolna neighbourhood of Józsefváros, such as the renewal of housing, streets and public spaces and the creation of a community centre, cannot hide local government intentions to change the neighbourhood's character and the composition of the present population. One aim is clearly to gradually push out visibly "problematic" social groups, poor Roma families in particular, by redrawing social and spatial borders between the different ethnic and social groups that live in Józsefváros. This is coupled with selective social policies that tend to criminalize and racialize of poverty. The impacts of such practices can only be assessed in the long term. However, such re-bordering attempts could undermine any sense of solidarity with poor and particular Roma and open the way for gentrification to transform the area.

## Everyday bordering and place-making

Within the context of this discussion, bordering can be defined as a situational process of negotiating social contexts that at the same time involves spatial bounding (see Kolossov and Scott 2013). Borders are an attempt to suggest edges and limits and to construct a degree of order within "unordered" situations. At the same time these limits often remain fuzzy and indeterminate and thus contentious. Borders involve differentiation, filtering and control practices, but also hybridization and border-crossing inventiveness (Brambilla 2014). As Kramsch (2002) argues, borders do not necessarily support an exclusive use or meaning of space and place, they can also sustain interdependence, negotiation and adaptation. These tension-laden qualities of borders are intrinsic to the social production of space and it is therefore crucial to revisit them in terms of a deeper understanding of place-making processes and their social and political consequences.

Following our constructivist lines of interpretation ethnicity is not an objective, permanent category, conceived as a matter of relations between predefined, fixed groups, but rather a process of constituting and reconfiguring groups by defining boundaries between them. Ethnicity and hence socio-ethnic borders may encompass different meanings in various contexts that change over time, often due to overarching socio-economic or political contexts (Brubaker 2004). Ethnic boundaries are also an outcome of the classificatory struggles and negotiations between actors situated in social fields characterized by institutional orders, distributions of power and political networks (Lamont and Molnár 2002; Wimmer 2008). In Hungary and other Central European countries Roma are extremely heterogeneous with regard to language, traditions, subsistence strategies and levels of social inclusion (Havas 1989; Tremlett 2014). Nevertheless, dominant representations of Roma in Hungary reduce this social complexity, maintaining notions of "gypsyness" that reflect the perceptions and imaginaries of mainstream (non-Roma) society. In this way, symbolic and physical boundaries serve to perpetuate unequal social and power relations and different forms of exclusion (McGarry 2014; Váradi and Virág 2014).

Urban settings are laboratories that offer insights into how borders are created within society in different social, ethnic, cultural and political circumstances. Cities are themselves much more than materializations of economic relations, they can be more generally understood as products of border-making processes, composed of a mosaic of interlinked yet differentiated spaces that give a particular city its social, economic, cultural and political character. Our theorizations of bordering involve a potentially wide field of social practices that directly relate to urban place-making. In studying the condition of Roma communities in Budapest we will largely focus on the local-level and on social bordering processes as part of the "practice of everyday life". Inspired by de Certeau's (1980) now classic analytical vision, everyday bordering describes specific ways of maintaining, controlling but also transforming social space through material and discursive means. On this view, strategies designed to organize space and to impose a specific narrative and image of place are confronted by tactics that subvert and re-appropriate place identities. de Certeau's perspective has been applied quite productively in discussions of formal state or state-like borders (Nugent 2011; Ward, Silberman, and Till 2012). However, despite some important exceptions (Kokalanova 2009; Breitung 2011; Iossifova 2015) the urban context of de Certeau's actual field of study has been somewhat neglected. Following de Certeau's perspective and understanding borders as open-ended *bordering* processes rather than finalizable institutions (Scott 2012), social borders emerge as narratives, as stories that develop through interactions in space that give meaning to urban place (Egger 2012). The borders of places, such as neighbourhoods, are therefore constructed and communicated by different representations of places and uses of physical space. As a result, borders create place images and identities while the city is itself intimately tied to the politics of representation (Smith 2005) which can involve the construction of alternative images and boundaries of urban space.

As the above suggests, bordering urban spaces often involves a tension between "official" and instrumental forms of place-making and informal, everyday narratives of place. One aspect of formal bordering is the use of sanctions by public actors in order to control access to urban spaces (Wacquant 2009). By controlling urban spaces, for example by excluding and sanctioning homeless people, urban politics ensure both a liveable environment for "law abiding" citizens, and value capture for urban rehabilitation and capital investments (Mitchell 2003; Misetics 2013). Furthermore, urban redevelopment often destroys existing borders (e.g. as expressed by buildings, roads, physical barriers, poor and "dangerous" neighbourhoods) in order to connect subareas of the city as consumption and residential spaces (Spierings 2012). Informal bordering processes on the other hand often compete with, and even subvert, elite-led appropriations of place identities and images. To paraphrase Smith (2002), such bordering processes often involve "localization" in which community is both locally defined but also connected to wider social contexts through a variety of performative and symbolic means.

Consequently, representations of places within a given urban context reflect shifting relationships between decision-makers, the majority population, the poor and questions of belonging and ethnicity that surface in local practice, discourse and policies. Our study of socio-ethnic dynamics of urban regeneration and its impacts on Roma communities will relate everyday social bordering to place-making and *the politics of representation* that these processes reflect. And indeed, boundary-making processes are central to interpretations of Roma discrimination in Budapest because they link localized place-making with the more global contextual framing of Hungary's Roma communities. The boundary-making process is itself highly political, both from a formal and an informal point of view as it involves a spatialized politics that conditions the social visibility of Roma communities. However, it is also a manifestation of local appropriations of space and of belonging and makes apparent the vicissitudes of top-down intervention in urban regeneration. In terms of methodology, we have pursued a strategy of targeting actors and positions that reflect the intersectional complexity of Józsefváros. In terms of interviews, we have thus interacted with social workers, activists, representatives of various Roma organizations and other informed social agents who confront poverty, Roma community concerns and problems of socio-ethnic marginalization. In addition, we have contrasted these positions with those of the official face of regeneration in the VIII District. Stakeholder interaction required us to actively follow social media and the activities of local citizens' groups. Our analysis was also based on a review of relevant literature, interviews with informed researchers and participant observation of different public events in the neighbourhood. These events included public forums and hearings for local inhabitants, conferences, participatory planning meetings, as well as protests against evictions.

As Yin (2003, 10) has stated: "case studies [...] are generalizable to theoretical propositions and not to populations or universes". Following this understanding we elaborate here a single revelatory case in terms of linking public policies, bordering processes and Roma marginalization. The area we have studied has been subject since the early 2000s to a long-term regeneration strategy. Its value as a case study is enhanced by the fact that it has been showcased as a new paradigm in Central and East European urban regeneration policies which, in contrast to outright demolition and more heavy-handed approaches to the treatment of poorer residents, Roma families in particular, has (at least theoretically) strived for cohesion and social sustainability. In the following we will portray the development of Józsefváros since 1990 in terms of a contested politics of representation, emphasizing interconnections between narratives representing the neighbourhood, the place-making actions and policies undertaken by different actors and stakeholders, reactions to these narratives and the results they have achieved. Ultimately, politics of representation are about visibility and the making (in)visible of specific socio-ethnic contexts. As we will demonstrate, political, economic, social, cultural actors have been reshaping the neighbourhood's image by addressing popular narratives of poverty and Roma "ghettoization" – either by emphasizing them, turning them into positive messages or by trying to change them according to specific interests and perspectives.

## The Magdolna Quarter: a site of urban regeneration and place-making

Before 1945 living in Józsefváros meant a kind of "decent poverty" (Gyáni 1992). Local society was heterogeneous and despite spatial separation in terms of employment, ethnicity and religion, there was no real social segregation. In the written history of the district, Roma do not appear as an independent social group and a Roma presence in Józsefváros can only be reconstructed from individual recollections, such as this passage from Péliné's (1996, 69) autobiographical novel:

> Józsefváros is unique, and it is where most of Roma live. [ ... ] This house was inhabited by rather shabby people. There were peasants, Roma, and Jews living there, but we lived in complete harmony. [ ... ] Somehow poverty kept the people together. [ ... ] Being Roma, Jewish or Hungarian was never subject to discussion, and it never even emerged as an idea.

Starting in the 1960s the social composition and status of Józsefváros radically changed and the district began to be associated both with poverty and with Roma communities. On the one hand, due to the social and ethnic policy of State Socialism, best summarized as a forced emancipation, Roma inclusion was effectively tied to an obligation to work. However, the economic role of Roma was primarily limited to unskilled labour which assured continued discrimination and segregation, linking Roma ethnicity to urban poverty and second-rate citizenship (Szalai 2000). On the other hand, state socialist policies also prompted the migration of rural Roma to the rapidly developing capital city and, ultimately, to run-down central districts. The highly centralized and bureaucratic housing allocation system reserved substandard public housing of Józsefváros for large low-income families, assuming their inability to cover the costs of newer flats in this district (Ladányi 1989, 1992; Zolnay 1993). At the same time, higher status inhabitants began to leave Józsefváros.

By the political transition of the 1990s, Józsefváros had become a neighbourhood sharply different from those surrounding it, characterized by both spatial and social segregation. Particularly affected was the area of Józsefváros situated outside the inner-city ring which came to be seen by majority society as the "Harlem of Pest", an urban imaginary based on racialized stereotypes and popular images of a Roma ghetto despite the fact that the majority population was and remains mostly non-Roma. The relative isolation and stigmatization of these neighbourhoods has been the result of a complex and long-term process, a cumulative product of political and social transformation that began during state socialism and that has continued to the present day (Kovács 2009). Moreover, these neighbourhoods have become obstacles to further development of the district in that they represent strong visual and perceptual boundaries, contrasting starkly with adjacent inner-city areas of renovation and gentrification. Józsefváros' decline has elicited policy responses and consciousness-raising on the part of local decision-makers and civil society actors. Since the turn of millennium, the need to counter the stigmatization of the district and thus break down physical, cultural and mental borders between these areas and the other parts of the city have become an objective shared by different stakeholders. Various initiatives reflect the common purpose of re-bordering Józsefváros' deprived neighbourhoods – that is, integrating them within the overall development of the city but also providing them a sense of positive distinction. Nevertheless, the place-making actions undertaken during the last ten to fifteen years have reflected very different policies and positions and as such have led to the formulation of very diverse narratives and images of the area.

Because of its paradigmatic nature, the so-called Magdolna Quarter deserves particular attention. This area has been developed since the early 2000s as part of a long-term regeneration strategy in contrast to outright demolition and more heavy-handed approaches to the treatment of poorer residents (Fayman, Keresztély, and Tomay 2008; RESPECT 2010). With much of the housing stock of substandard quality, Magdolna was designated as a pilot project of social urban renewal in Budapest and in 2005 the government of the VIII District launched the first phase of the Magdolna Neighbourhood Urban Renewal Programme (MNP), co-financed by the district and the city of Budapest and European Union support. The basic concept of MNP has followed several Western European examples of socially integrative urban regeneration initiatives, such as the case of Birmingham, or the Soziale Stadt programme in Germany (Fayman, Keresztély, and Tomay 2008). In line with these examples, the goal of MNP has been to develop an integrated and socially mixed neighbourhood, and to encourage local people to participate in the development of the local community. In doing this, MNP aims to improve the quality of life in the area as well as promote small-scale private investment (Keresztély and Scott 2012).

Although never openly emphasized, one main goal of MNP has always been the eradication of the neighbourhood's image as a Roma ethnic ghetto. The official place-making strategies of the VIII District have, despite different ideological positions and understandings of integration, all strived for a "normalization" of the Magdolna's image and a reconfiguration of the local population in order to create a more mainstream, "socially compatible" neighbourhood environment. However, implementation to this goal has reflected different ideological and social approaches. For instance, the ruling political elites have always promoted the image of a regenerated neighbourhood – although this regeneration has been conceived in different forms, according to the political leanings of local government. Parallel to this, Roma activists have attempted to transcend received notions of "ghetto" and recast their neighbourhoods as places where Roma culture and belonging can be expressed and experienced. Indeed, there has also been a conversion of sorts of the negative image of ghetto into a space of urban coolness, partly through the actions of local Roma youth but also by outsiders who have discovered Magdolna and other areas of the VIII District (György 2009; Imre 2009). All of this indicates that the question of transforming public perceptions of the District's neighbourhoods has involved several contesting representations that oscillate between a zone of multicultural integration (and a pioneer project of citizen participation), a performative space for the promotion of Roma pride and belonging, and a highly normative vision of social order targeted at the endorsement of "mainstream" society.

### Politics of representation – framing the multicultural neighbourhood

A major regeneration narrative of Józsefváros and the Magdolna Quarter is one of transformation from an isolated Roma ghetto to an attractive multi-ethnic neighbourhood. In this place-making vision, a lively and multicultural urban environment is emerging that despite its social problems and tensions is a source of strength, reinforcing the cosmopolitan character of the capital city. This image is reinforced by major redevelopment and improvement pro-jects bordering the Magdolna: the entertainment, retailing and housing complex of the Corvin Promenade, the elegant Palace Quarter and the faculty of Kandó Kálmán University. At the same time, the Magdolna Quarter itself is represented as the socially sensitive face of Józsefváros' transformation, an example of comprehensive community regeneration that emulates European best practices (Tosics 2015). One Roma rights activist and social worker stated in an interview that:

> Working in the VIIIth district had always meant for me crossing the street and entering to the Syrian hairdresser to agree with him on my new hairstyle; then going out for lunch at the Chinese; than saying hello to the Arab baker and exchanging a few words with him about the weather. I had the feeling of being in a small provincial town. It was very interesting to see that Chinese families took Roma nurses to their children, that Roma women made the house-work for them.

Within the context of these "multiculturalist" urban regeneration policies, representations of Józsefváros, and the Magdolna neighbourhood in particu-lar, have reflected the presence of Roma in rather ambiguous ways. One the one hand, the treatment of their everyday material problems has been reduced, once again, to a question of poverty and social inequalities rather than related to identity issues. In this sense, the Magdolna programme has been officially framed as "colour-blind" and place-based, downplaying Roma ethnicity as a neighbourhood-defining element. On the other hand, cul-tural and educational aspects of MNP have highlighted the significance of Roma culture within a vision of a special multi-ethnic neighbourhood, following similar examples from all over Europe. This development can be clearly perceived through the transformations which have occurred in the functioning and leadership of the Neighbourhood Community Centre, one of the main tools realized within the MNP in order to enhance social integration. The Centre was created by the conversion of a former Gloves Factory situated in Mátyás square. The refurbishment of the building was realized during MNP1, while the cultural concept and the realization of the programmes were organized during MNP2. Between 2008 and 2011, the centre enjoyed considerable financial and operational autonomy. During the first phase, the work of the Community Centre was informed by a vision of multicultural local community and was aimed at facilitating the integration of Roma through different cultural, educational and social programmes. The method was to involve local NGOs in order to respond to real local needs and create a wide variety of programmes that would attract and bring together both Roma and non-Roma residents.

Unsurprisingly, integration, at least as originally conceived, has been elusive. For example, Roma and non-Roma inhabitants rarely attended the same community-oriented programmes. The only real occasions for interaction have been those of street festivals and concerts, organized in cooperation with local NGOs. While these events were not really local ones and or socially representative – they attracted a large number of young people, artistes etc. from all parts of Budapest – they greatly increased the general visibility of the neighbourhood and its multicultural nature. Still, social and ethnic barriers and hence segregation between the different groups in the neighbourhood have remained the rule. The externally applied, that is, "European", place narrative of multiculturalism has been rather employed as a place-making slogan and the appropriation of Roma cultures and identities used rather as an expedient that has skirted messy issues of everyday stigmatization of poorer Roma families and youth. This interpretation of gentrified multiculturalism contrasts starkly with a notion of neighbourhood oriented towards satisfying basic needs. As one Roma rights activist exclaimed in an interview:

> [...] in case of discriminatory policies, political power can easily find the Gypsies, but in the case of policies needed to allocate equal rights for the Roma, political power often argues that it is legally impossible to define who is Roma and who is not.

### Roma belonging, Roma pride

This multicultural bordering and place narrative has coexisted, often uncomfortably, with an alternative strategy of Roma visibility representing the Magdolna Quarter and other areas of Józsefváros, as a locus of belonging, community development and improvement. Beginning in the early 1990s,

Roma groups consisting mainly of trained musicians embarked on an attempt to improve the status of the neighbourhood. They were among the instigators in establishing and operating numerous Roma educational and cultural institutions and civil rights movements. In the early years of the political transition, Józsefváros, and especially the area that later became the Magdolna neighbourhood, developed as the centre of national level institutions representing Roma culture and Roma society. In the 1990s, national Roma policy was closely linked to the most powerful Roma NGO known as the "Roma Parliament" which enjoyed solid political ties with the liberal leadership of the district, and as such reinforced the political position of the Roma minority in Józsefváros. The Parliament operated as an umbrella organization and besides provided active political representation regularly offered musical and theatrical events too, as well as the first, and only, permanent exhibition of contemporary Roma art and a Roma cultural periodical Amaro Drom. It also operated a social and legal protection service offering assistance primarily, though not exclusively, to the Roma inhabitants of the district.

Thanks to its Roma and non-Roma cultural programmes, the Roma Parliament grew not only into a major institution of Roma representation, but into an important cultural centre for other intellectuals as well. It maintained close ties to other associations and initiatives such as the Roma community centre, the primary school Roma clubs, the Józsefváros theatre which staged regular talk shows with Roma artists, and the Roma Civil Rights Foundation (Roma Polgárjogi Alapítvány) created in 1995 primarily for preventing evictions of Roma people all over in the country. Radio C, a Roma community channel covering all Budapest, also started operations in the same area in 2000. All these institutions, mutually reinforcing each another, helped produce the image of a large Roma presence in the VIII District. These appropriations of neighbourhood as a space of Roma belonging have not always meshed with the multicultural narrative of "new" Józsefváros. The MNP has had difficulty in reconciling its mission of social equity and sustainability with highly negative perceptions of everyday Roma culture. While Roma institutions and organizations have relieved some of the isolation of families living here and helped them in solving their problems, they also have contributed to the high visibility of Roma in Józsefváros and in this way, ironically if not cruelly, reinforced popular perceptions of the District as an "ethnic ghetto".

### Contingent integration and a punitive turn

In 2010 a right-wing political majority within city government took power. This change meant the reinforcing of place-making strategies seeking to de-emphasize multiculturalism and neighbourhood ethnic identities and instead focus on showcase projects of redevelopment on the one hand (e.g. under the slogan of "Józsefváros rebuilds") and social welfare and public order on the other. At the same time, the goal of supporting gentrification tendencies already present in the area became more apparent. As part of this shift the new local government also reduced the power and autonomy of the MNP's leadership and the public company (RÉV8) responsible for implementation. Project management was directly incorporated into municipal governance structures and the number of employees considerably reduced. As for the Community Centre its leadership was relieved of management tasks within RÉV8 and everyday running of the Centre became part of local government.

The Community Centre's new leadership duly adopted the new approach to social cohesion in the Magdolna area with a place-making narrative that was decisively traditionalist, based on a top-down and prescriptive integration of the Roma community into majority society. Through the new administrative structures, the Community Centre began to function as a municipal institution for services such as job-seeking assistance and training for the unemployed, but programmes that targeted cultural issues, for example through neighbourhood events, were eliminated. In an interview conducted by the authors, the Centre's director stated that: "we are not a centre for Roma cultural integration" and "we are definitely not a place for organizing parties". In this way, the period of experimenting with local and decentralized cultural projects of social integration ended after 2011.

## A racial turn

This new approach of the MNP and the Community Centre's work reflects the change of paradigm, a turn from a vision based on a multiculturalism and integrated development towards a notion of neighbourhood where values and rules are defined solely by the majority society and by personal choices. Parallel to the exclusion of NGOs connected previously to MNP2 was the conscious weakening of the Roma Parliament and other organizations of Roma representation. At one point the local government considered the highly symbolic act of re-appropriating the building housing the Roma Parliament and thus forcing the organization to move. This move would have in fact facilitated the renewal of public spaces according to the MNP. Renovating this part of the Magdolna neighbourhood, and turning it into a pedestrian precinct, has linked it to the elegant and gentrified district of the neighbouring Palotanegyed (Palace District). This concept was visually, even architecturally, reinforced by the use of identical paving and street furniture in the two quarters. There are two important institutions in the same street: the faculty of the University and the Roma Parliament; while the former dovetails with the gentrification endeavours in progress in the district, the function of the latter is not in line with the concept. Thanks to the efforts of civil activists and organizations, the Roma Parliament remained, although the role of the organization itself has been considerably reduced.

The case of the Roma Parliament highlights another important issue: as in political and public discourse where racism has greatly increased since the mid-2000s, solidarity with vulnerable social and ethnic groups has weakened. From the mid-2000s there has been a racial turn in mainstream discourses and in certain policy areas (social protection, welfare, labour and later education policies) (Vidra and Fox 2014). The rise of radical racist discourses, coupled with the political successes of the radical right, have set the political and media agenda by again raising the "Roma question" in which Roma appear as annoying beggars, welfare dependents, prostitutes and thieves. The flip side of this representation is the figure of the Roma musician serving and born to entertain the majority society as an accessory of the latter (Kóczé and Trehan 2009). The representation of the romantic figure of the Roma musician reinforces the romantic image of an era long gone – a representation accurately fitting the current government's nostalgic interpretation of the pre-Second World War period – and neglects the linguistic, cultural and social diversity of the Roma society and the emancipatory endeavours of the past decades. With a considerable degree of resignation, one interviewed Roma sociologist and local activist exclaimed that

> there are two accepted Roma roles [for integrating into majority society]: one of them is managing otherwise non-efficient social programmes, the other one is being a Roma musician and playing at representative events. Politicians and public discourse take advantage of both of them.

This new image is promoted specifically by the VIII District's local government and a freshly created Roma cultural centre closely cooperates with it. In addition, a "Park of Roma Musicians" was inaugurated – albeit on a rather hidden street. The cultural centre sustains a musical group, the Józsefváros Roma Band, mostly as part of a public employment scheme, and organizes an annual Roma Music Festival that features "traditional" Roma music at various public places of the district.

### Penal populism

This paradigm shift in representing the neighbourhood has also been accompanied by a punitive turn – a penalization of poverty (Wacquant 2009) and a criminalization of homelessness. These policies are signs of a deep structural and political crisis in Hungary. The assertion of power through *penal populism* has gained ground and resulted in increased social tensions. While the current punitive surge has its antecedents in the neoliberal policies of past governments (Misetics 2013), the criminalization of homelessness and drug abuse treatment (!) has now become systematic and volunteer movements that assist marginalized groups are facing increasing pressure. These new policies have also fed into a popular narrative of Gypsy crime and have thus targeted poor Roma families and homeless as well. Criminalization and an increase in the number of local police has forced drug use, homelessness and prostitution into dilapidated buildings of former industrial areas. This increasingly concentrates neighbourhood problems in a relatively restricted geographical space (Ráczet al. 2010). At the same time, however, a significant part of the District has been "cleansed" of persons seen as deviant or socially undesirable.

As in many cities housing policies in Budapest constitute one of the main urban regeneration tools that facilitate the exclusion of criminalized and problematic social groups. Exclusion has been a problematic aspect of the regeneration programme since its beginnings in 2005, although in its first phases it was compensated by general objectives supporting integrated community development. Since the advent of right-wing political leadership the wholesale change of population has been clearly articulated as a political objective (see also above). This policy can clearly be detected in the district housing polices, including that of MNP, which in large part are based on managing social housing that is comparatively abundant in Józsefváros and in the Magdolna area in particular. A large sector of the tenants is trapped within a spiral of indebtedness, and an inability to pay bills and rent often leads to eviction and ultimately exclusion from the social welfare system (Horváth and Pósfai 2014). The number of these renters at risk is permanently increasing and according to the observations of housing rights activists and other experts, a considerable percentage of them are of Roma origin. Thus, although it has never been officially admitted, the Roma population have always been particularly affected by housing policies that target exclusion. Supporting these affected groups had in fact been the main objective of the Roma Rights Protection offices that was hosted by the Roma Parliament until 2011.

At the same time, the policy of eviction contradicts the main objectives of the MNP which is financed by the European Union as a programme enhancing social integration and urban regeneration without displacement. The contradiction has become particularly evident during the third phase of MNP, when after the launching of the financing period an extra element was added to the programme by the municipality, the complete renovation of ten "crisis buildings". According to municipal decision, these buildings have been selected according to the following criteria: (1) tenants are characterized by typical problems of anti-social behaviour and incapacity to live within the community; (2) the buildings and their environment are particularly affected by the possibility of crime; (3) tenants with rent arrears are overrepresented (4) the number of illegal occupants is higher than the average. Crisis buildings are thus spaces where "problematic groups", including many Roma families, are concentrated – in fact forcibly moved to – before the start of construction work. Very probably these persons will never be able to resettle to newly renovated flats due to higher rental and energy costs.

As a final observation, it must be noted that in contrast to more recent shifts towards highly conservative, normative and punitive approaches to neighbourhood development, new forms of Roma representation have emerged through informal channels. These new movements have been largely based on the use of social media, such as Facebook and Twitter. The "We Belong Here Movement" was formed in the year of the national census (2011) with the aim of persuading Romani people to openly declare their Roma identity. After the census was completed, the movement remained active as a virtual community serving local Roma communities, organizing civil rights actions and different cultural events such as the Roma Pride Day and Roma Resistance Day, not only in the Magdolna neighbourhood but also in different locations around the country. These can be considered good examples of reactive ethnic mobilization in a new, changing political environment (Setét 2013). Apart from this virtual organization, Gallery8, the contemporary Roma gallery established in 2010 at Mátyás square, is presently the only institution to represent the social and cultural identity of the Roma living in the neighbourhood. In addition to art exhibitions, Gallery8 undertakes the mission of representing the social problems of disadvantaged minorities by placing its exhibitions in an international context, connected to civil rights movements and to the sociological concept of "critical whiteness" (Junghaus 2011).

## Conclusions

Bordering is an everyday process of creating distinction and maintaining a sense of identity, often in conjunction with place attachments. In our case study area, which involved the regeneration of the Budapest's Magdolna neighbourhood, bordering could, furthermore, be observed as a multilevel process, influenced by national politics, local policies and persistent popular stereotypes but also by local actors creating public spaces for the articulation of community needs. Consequently, we have focused on tensions between politically instrumentalized appropriations of Roma identity and Roma attempts to re-appropriate local space as an empowering environment and facilitator of a sense of belonging.

What appears clear is that multicultural and normative-contingent approaches to integration and neighbourhood development have favoured, first of all, gentrification processes that inherently serve to divide the Roma community and marginalize the poorest neighbourhood residents. These bordering processes have generated several new forms of exclusion in the area, clearly contradicting the EU's goals of promoting social cohesion and cultural tolerance and suggesting a rather cynical implementation of EU structural and other public funds. These place-making strategies have also contributed to the generation of new borders in the area. Physical borders have emerged between the streets, facades and the inner courtyards, between the rehabilitated streets and the dilapidated ones, between the rehabilitated areas and the steadily shrinking slum and "ghetto" area. Social borders have been accentuated between old and new inhabitants, Roma and non-Roma, and, ultimately between "good" and "undesirable" Roma and thus also within Roma society itself.

As the above discussion has suggested, bordering, for example as place-making, involves making "visible", both physically and discursively, specific narratives and appropriations of neighbourhood space. In the case of the VIII District, the Magdolna Quarter in particular, local appropriations of neighbourhood space have often diverged from those characterized by the rationalities of government. Indeed, the Roma community's own representations of the neighbourhood have provided powerful counter-narratives. This has included the promotion of a sense of Roma pride as an alternative to mainstream policies of integration. Ultimately, however, these attempts at place-making reflect the problematic legacy of Roma discrimination and the difficulty of creating a more generally empowering environment for Roma communities.

## Acknowledgements

The authors would like to thank our colleagues within the EUBORDERSCAPES project, Nira Yuval-Davis, Georgie Wemyss and Kathryn Cassidy in particular, for support and critical feedback. In addition we would like to acknowledge the informed criticisms and comments provided by the reviewers.

## Disclosure statement

No potential conflict of interest was reported by the authors.

## Funding

This article is based on research funded by the European Union's Seventh Framework Programme for Research and Technological Development within the scope of the EUBORDERSCAPES project [grant number 290775].

## References

Brambilla, C. 2014. "Exploring the Critical Potential of the Borderscapes Concept." *Geopolitics* 20 (1): 1–21.

Breitung, W. 2011. "Borders and the City: Intra-urban Boundaries in Guangzhou (China)." *Quaestiones Geographicae* 30 (4): 55–61.

Brubaker, R. 2004. *Ethnicity Without Groups*. Cambridge, MA: Harvard University Press.

de Certeau, M. 1980. *L' invention du Quotidien. 1. les arts de faire* [The Invention of the Everyday. The Art of Doing Things]. Paris: Gallimard.

Egger, R. 2012. "Borders as Narratives." In *Transnational Spaces and Regional Localizations*, edited by A. Pilch Ortega, and B. Schröttner, 105–116. Münster: Waxmann.

Fayman, S., K. Keresztély, and K. Tomay. 2008. *Le politiques de renouvellement urbain des villes d'Europe central illustrées pour le réhabilitation des quartiers existants: La ville de de Budapest en Hongrie* [Politics of Urban Renewal in Central European Cities as Exemplified by the Rehabilitation of Existing Neighbourhoods: The Case of Budapest, Hungary]. Paris: Agence Nationale de l'Habitation.

Gyáni, G. 1992. *Bérkaszárnya és nyomortelep* [Tenement and Slum]. Budapest: Magvető Könyvkiadó.

György, E. 2009. "'Nyócker': Egy negyed mint reprezentációs hely" [Nyócker: A Neighbourhood as Representational Space]. *Budapesti Negyed* 17 (1): 149–161.

Havas, G. 1989. "A cigány közösségek történeti típusairól" [Historical Typologies of Roma Communities]. *Kultúra és Közösség* 16 (4): 3–17.

Horváth, V., and Z. S. Pósfai. 2014. "Ma Magyarországon lakhatási válság van" [There is a Present Housing Crisis in Hungary]. *Heti Világgazdaság* March 21, 2014. http://hvg. hu/itthon/2 0 1 4 0 3 2 1 _Ma_Magyarorszagon_lakhatasi_valsag_van.

van Houtum, H., O. T. Kramsch, and W. Zierhofer. 2005. *Bordering Space*. Aldershot: Ashgate.

Imre, A. 2009. *Identity Games*. Cambridge: MIT Press.

Iossifova, D. 2015. "Borderland Urbanism: Seeing Between Enclaves." *Urban Geography* 36 (1): 90–108.

Junghaus, T. 2011. "A fehérség kritikai kutatása." http://tranzit.blog.hu/2011/08/01/a_ feherseg_kritikai_kutatasa_critical_whiteness_studies_i.

Keresztély, K., and J. W. Scott. 2012. "Urban Regeneration in the Post-socialist Context: Budapest and the Search for a Social Dimension." *European Planning Studies* 20 (7): 1111–1134.

Kóczé, A., and N. Trehan. 2009. "Postcolonial Racism and Social Justice: The Struggle for the Soul of Romani Civil Rights Movement in the 'New Europe'." In *Racism, Post-colonialism*, edited by G. Huggan, 50–77. Liverpool: Liverpool University Press.

Kokalanova, A. 2009. "Dealing with Urban Borders The Example of the Border between the Fakulteta Segregated Ethnic Roma Settlement and the Rest of Sofia." Paper presented at the International RC21 Conference 2013. http://www.rc21.org/ conferences/berlin2013/RC21-Berlin-Papers-2/04-1-Kokalanova.pdf.

Kolossov, V., and J. W. Scott. 2013. "Selected Conceptual Issues in Border Studies." *Belgeo. Revue belge de géographie* 1: 1–19. http://belgeo.revues.org/10532.

Kovács, Z. 2009. "Social and Economic Transformation of Historical Neighbourhoods in Budapest." *Tijdschrift voor Economische en Sociale Geografie* 100 (4): 399–416.

Kramsch, O. T. 2002. "Reimagining the Scalar Topologies of Cross-Border Governance: Eu(ro) Regions in the Post-colonial Present." *Space and Polity* 6 (2): 169–196.

Ladányi, J. 1989. "Changing Patterns of Residential Segregation in Budapest." *International Journal of Urban and Regional Research* 13 (4): 555–572.

Ladányi, J. 1992. "Gondolatok a Középső-Józsefváros Rehabilitációjának Társadalmi Összefüggéseiről." *Tér és Társadalom* 3–4: 75–88.

Lamont, M., and V. Molnár. 2002. "The Study of Boundaries in the Social Sciences." *Annual Review of Sociology* 28: 167–195.

McGarry, A. 2014. "Roma as a Political Identity: Exploring Representations of Roma in Europe." *Ethinicities* 14 (6): 756–774.

Misetics, B. 2013. "The Criminalization of Homelessness in Hungary." In *Mean Streets. A Report on Criminalization of Homelessness in Europe*, edited by S. Jones, 101–112. Brussels: Housing Rights Watch.

Mitchell, D. 2003. *The Right to the City. Social Justice and the Fight for Public Space.* New York: Guilford Press.

Nugent, P. 2011. "Bourdieu and De Certeau at the Border Post: Trans-boundary Communities, Government Officials and Everyday Life in West Africa." In *Auf dem Boden der Tatsachen: Festschrift fur Thomas Bierschenk*, edited by N. Schareika, E. Spies, and P.-Y. Le Meur, 361–376. Koln: Rudiger Koeppe Verlag.

Péliné, N. H. 1996. *Az én kis életem* [About My Little Life]. Budapest: T-Twins Kiadó.

Rácz, J., F. Márványkövi, K. Melles, and V. Vadász. 2010. *Út a túléléshez – Nyílt színi droghasználat és "belövőszobák" Budapesten Az ártalomcsökkentéssel kapcsolatos megfontolások* [Road to survival – The Open Drug Scene and Shooting Galleries in Budapest. Recommendations for Harm Reduction]. Budapest: L' Harmattan Kiadó.

RESPECT. 2010. "Urban Reconstruction, Social Exclusion and the Roma in Bundapest." Workshop at the Central European University, November 19. Report of the RESPECT project, funded by the Seventh Framework Programme. Budapest: Central European University.

Rhodes, J. 2012. "Stigmatization, Space and Boundaries in De-Industrial Burnley." *Ethnic and Racial Studies* 35 (4): 684–703.

Scott, J. W. 2012. "European Politics of Borders, Border Symbolism and Cross-Border Cooperation." In *A Companion to Border Studies*, edited by T. Wilson, and H. Donnan, 83–99. Hobolen: Wiley-Blackwell.

Setét, J. 2013. "Akkor is cigány vagyok" [I am Still a Gypsy]. 2000 *Irodalmi és társadalmi havilap* 2013. 4. http://ketezer.hu/2013/10/akkor-is-cigany-vagyok-2/.

Smith, N. 1996. *The New Urban Frontier: Gentrification and the Revanchist City.* New York: Routledge.

Smith, M. P. 2002. "Power in Place: Re-theorizing the Local and the Global." In *Understanding the City: Contemporary and Future Perspectives*, edited by J. Eade, and C. Mele, 109–130. London: Blackwell.

Smith, M. P. 2005. "Power in Place. Contextualising Transnational Research." *City and Society* 17 (1): 5–34.

Spierings, B. 2012. "Economic Flows, Spatial Folds and Intra-urban Borders: Reflections on City Centre Redevelopment Plans from a European Border Studies Perspective." *Tijdschrift Voor Economische en Sociale Geografie* 103 (1): 110–117.

Szalai, J. 2000. "Az elismerés politikája és a 'cigánykérdés'. A többségi-kisebbségi viszony néhány jelenkori problémájáról" [Politics of Recognition and the "Gypsy Question". Contemporary Questions of Majority-Minority Relations]." In *Cigánynak születni* [Born as a Gypsy], edited by A. Horváth, E. Landau, and J. Szalai, 531–572. Budapest: Új Mandátum Könyvkiadó.

Tosics, I. 2015. "Housing Renewal in Hungary. From Socialist Non-intervention, Through Individual Market Actions to Area-based Public Intervention." In *Renewing Europe's Housing*, edited by R. Turkington, and C. Watson, 161–187. Bristol: Policy Press.

Tremlett, A. 2014. "Making a Difference Without Creating a Difference: Super-diversity as a New Direction for Research on Roma Minorities." *Ethnicities* 14 (6): 830–848.

Váradi, M., and T. Virág. 2014. "Faces and Causes of Roma Marginalization. Experiences from Hungary." In *Faces and Causes of Roma Marginalization in Local Contexts: Hungary, Romania, Serbia*, edited by J. Szalai, and V. Zentai, 35–65. Budapest:

Central European University. http://pasos.org/wp-content/uploads/2015/01/cps-book-faces-and-causes-2014.pdf.

Vidra, Z. S., and J. Fox. 2014. "Mainstreaming of Racist Anti-Roma Discourses in the Media in Hungary." *Journal of Immigrant and Refugee Studies* 12 (4): 437–455.

Wacquant, L. 2009. *Punishing the Poor. The Neoliberal Government of Social Insecurities*. Durham, NC: Duke University Press.

Ward, J., M. Silberman, and K. E. Till, eds. 2012. *Walls, Borders, Boundaries: Spatial and Cultural Practices in Europe*. New York: Berghahn Books.

Wimmer, A. 2008. "The Making and Unmaking of Ethnic Boundaries." *American Journal of Sociology* 113 (4): 970–1022.

Yin, R. K. 2003. *Case Study Research Design and Methods*. Thousand Oaks, CA: Sage.

Yuval-Davis, N. 2011. "Power, Intersectionality and the Politics of Belonging." (FREIA's tekstserie; No. 75). Aalborg: Institut for Kultur og Globale Studier, Aalborg Universitet. doi:10.5278/freia.58024502.

Yuval-Davis, N. 2015. "Situated Intersectionality and Social Inequality." *Raisons Politiques* 2: 91–100.

Zolnay, J. 1993. "A lakástörvény és a tulajdonviszonyok" [Housing Legislation and Ownership]. *Esély* 6: 97–108.

# Media mirrors? Framing Hungarian Romani migration to Canada in Hungarian and Canadian press

Viktor Varjú and Shayna Plaut

**ABSTRACT**

The most recent migration of Roma from Central-Eastern Europe to Canada started in the 1990s. Several thousand people from former socialist countries, including Hungarian Roma, moved overseas. There were many reasons but for Roma, the motivations not only included a drastic loss of employment, but re-emerging systemic and increasingly violent racism. This article focuses on the discursive framing of these motivations and the reaction within both Hungarian and Canadian newspapers from 1999 to 2013. In the article we show how the press engaged in framing and counter-framing the policies and politics of the host country through their coverage of "the Hungarian Roma" issue. Specifically, we focus on the differing and shifting spheres of consensus and the changing political/policy contexts by conducting an in-depth comparison of the changing media frames in Hungarian and Canadian newspaper coverage. We show how the "Hungarian Roma issue" becomes an example and reflection of the changing political culture.

## Introduction

According to the United Nation's Human Rights committee, the European Court of Human Rights and the Canadian Supreme Court, Roma in Europe face systemic and ongoing human rights violations in terms of employment, health, education and housing, as well as a real fear of physical violence. In addition the Central/Eastern states and everyday citizens have faced severe economic difficulties since the economic crisis and racism against Roma is increasing throughout the continent (Brown, Dweyer, and Scullion 2013; Engelhart 2013; Thelen 2005; UNDP 2003, 2011). These are the reasons that many Roma give when asked why they choose to leave their country of origin (Beaudoin, Danch, and Rehaag 2015).

50

There is nothing unique or new about individuals leaving their homeland based on fear or in search of a better life for their family. However, it has become evident that the folkloric stereotypes of the "wandering Gypsy" mean that Roma are facing very real and increased scrutiny by courts and immigration officials. This ethnic targeting is reflected, perpetuated and countered within the media discourse of the host countries.

Our article examines media coverage when large numbers of Roma from Hungary migrated to Canada claiming refugee status at the turn of the twenty-first century. As the "Background and context" sections argue, we selected the time frames of analysis based on changes within political-social realities of both Hungary and Canada including the imposition and lifting of visas for Hungarian nationals, increased violence against Roma in Hungary and the lead-up to legislation in Canada that included Hungary as a "safe country". As the "Methods and materials" shows, by conducting an in-depth comparison of the changing media frames in Hungarian and Canadian newspaper coverage, we applied a mixed methods analysis of 141 articles in six newspapers. By exploring both Hungarian and Canadian press during the same demarcated time periods in the "Results" section, we demonstrate how the press engaged in framing and counter-framing (Baer and Brysk 2009) of humanitarian, political, economic and nationalist discourses. In this section we identify particular patterns of what is deemed an "appropriate" narrative within different discursive spaces (Fraser 1991; Habermas [1964] 1974; Hallin 1994) and how this shifts. Recognizing that although journalists often envision themselves as "objective", in the "discussion", we argue that journalists themselves were actually advocating for various positions within a "sphere of consensus" (Hallin 1994). The "spheres of consensus" shifted based on the political/policy, economic and cultural contexts of their countries as well as the media's role within the countries (El-Nawawy and Iskandar 2002; Wade 2011). Thus we argue that "Romani migration" became both the symbol and the symptom of changing socio-political realities in both Hungary and Canada.

To be clear, Romani migration is not a new topic of scholarly inquiry. There is robust sociological and anthropological literature focused on emigration and immigration to Canada (Vidra 2013) or to other countries (Kováts 2002) as well as mass-media representation (Bernáth and Messing 2013), populism and extreme rights movements in Hungary (Vidra 2014). Our research is novel in its comparative dimension: we show how the "Hungarian Roma issue" becomes an example and reflection of the changing political culture of the host country.

## Background and context

### *Roma in Hungarian contexts*[1]

Definitions of who are Roma and what constitutes "legitimate Romani identity" are both varied and politically charged.[2] Due to the misuse of census data by the Nazi regime to commit genocide, many countries in Central and Eastern Europe did not collect ethnic data for decades. Although this has since changed, it is still quite sensitive (Durst 2010; OSF 2010; PER 2000). Because of the forced assimilation policies of Queen Maria Theresa to turn Roma into "new Magyars" fewer than twenty per cent of Roma in Hungary (including Boyash) speak Romani (Fraser 1995; Kemény 2000, 2005; Stewart 1997).

Under socialism, the treatment and living conditions of Hungarian Roma improved. Throughout the 1990s, Hungary was also seen as one of the pioneers of Romani rights – employing the first ever Romani self-government system in Europe, sending Romani MPs to the European Parliament and implementing positive discrimination measures. In addition, Hungary was home to the European Roma Rights Centre, Romani media outlets and other advocacy organizations (PER 2000; Pusca 2012). However, there was a marked difference between the formal positive rhetoric of the government and the deteriorating conditions on the ground. In the 1990s, economic and social situations began to deteriorate rapidly (Durst 2002). By 2011, sixty-one per cent of Roma women and forty-four per cent of Roma men were unemployed and there were ethnically targeted assaults throughout the country (Bernát 2014).

By the time of the 2008 economic crisis both the rhetoric and everyday reality disintegrated. Not only did the poor become poorer – at times destitute – but the gap between the rich and poor throughout Hungary increased drastically. After several years of disappointment in left-wing politics, voters in Hungary shifted towards the right. In 2010, left-wing parties lost the election and Fidesz (the right wing party) won two-thirds of Parliamentary seats granting it a "super majority" under Prime Minister Orbán. Concurrently, Jobbik, the far-right party, received twelve per cent of the votes in 2010 and twenty per cent in 2014 and Fidesz began co-opting some of its politics including its use of racism and fear. Terms such as "Gypsy crime" which had been unacceptable for decades were reintroduced and re-legitimized in the public and political discourse (Vidra 2014). With its "super majority", the second Orbán government began a rapid centralization process of governmental and media institutions which continues to the present (Bajomi-Lázár 2013). Due to this situation, trust in democratic effectiveness, as well as space for dissent, weakened (Bodor, Grünhut, and Horeczki 2014). As the monopoly over media increased, the practice of journalists changed: rather than actively "watchdogging" or criticizing governmental policies, journalists increasingly manifested their dissent by choosing to *not* cover the governmental party line. Opposition could be seen through silence.

### Changing politics of migration

With over sixty-five distinct Indigenous languages, Canada, has always been a culturally diverse place. As in all settler/colonial countries there were many attempts to eradicate, legislate and forcibly assimilate both Indigenous peoples and immigrants, particularly those from outside the British Empire (Gray 2011; Kymlicka 1995). Things changed in 1971 under Pierre Trudeau's government when the policy of "multiculturalism" was introduced and codified in the Multiculturalism Act of 1988. This value has become embedded in the national self-perception and promotion of Canada. In 2011, one out of five people in Canada were born abroad[3] and, according to the Mosaic Institute,[4] these "New Canadians" consistently rate "multiculturalism" as *the* cornerstone of Canadian identity.

Romani migration to Canada was recorded at the end of the nineteenth century, mostly from England and Russia. After the Second World War when new countries with strict political and nationalizing policies emerged, many ethnic minorities – including Roma – chose to leave Europe. In 1956 more than 37,000 refugees from Hungary, once again including Roma, came to Canada as political refugees fleeing the Soviet invasion (Arhin 2013).[5]

In 1994, Canada removed its visa requirement for Hungarian and Czech nationals. Although there was a major influx of Roma from the Czech Republic successfully claiming and receiving refugee status, there were few Hungarian nationals.[6] In 1998 the number of Hungarian refugee claims increased and in 1999, the Canadian Immigration and Refugee Board (IRB) decided to create a legal precedent – what they termed "lead case" – in order to provide guidance for similar cases.[7] Calling in Hungarian officials as well as the leader of the Hungarian Romani Self Government at the time, the Canadian immigration judges determined that although Roma suffer from discrimination in Hungary "this does not rise to the level of persecution".[8] In response, there was a much lower rate of acceptance but people still continued to file claims and in December 2001, the Canadian government reinstated the visa for Hungarian nationals (Arhin 2013; Beaudoin, Danch, and Rehaag 2015; Levine-Rasky, Beaudoin, and St Clair 2014).

Due to trade negotiations with the European Union and other bi-lateral agreements, in March 2008 Canada lifted its visa restriction against Hungarian nationals once again. As a result, the number of Hungarian refugee claims increased significantly the following year (Figure 1) (Arhin 2013).

In 2010, a human (labour) trafficking ring, the largest ever in Canada, was exposed. Both the ring leaders and victims were Hungarian Roma.[9] It was one of the first times that Roma were discussed as both potential victims and criminals within Canadian society. Within the post September 11th securitization framework, this human trafficking incident highlighted a conflation of refugees, immigration and criminality to the forefront of the Canadian political agenda and significant changes in Canadian immigration policy soon followed. In 2010, the Balanced Refugee Reform Bill (BillC11) passed in an attempt to address the three to five year backlog of refugee applicants. A

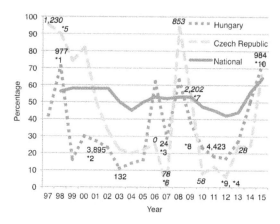

**Figure 1.** Acceptance rates for Hungarian and Czech Refugee Claimants Compared to National Acceptance Rates 1997–2015, with the number of claims and policy events for selected years.

Notes: *1 Hungary: Lead Case; *2 Hungary: Visa Imposed; *3 Hungary: Visa Lifted; *4 New Refugee Law; *5 Czech Republic: Visa Imposed; *6 Czech Republic: Visa Lifted; *7 Czech Republic: Visa Imposed; *8 "Bogus" remark; *9 Czech Republic: Visa Lifted; *10 New government

Figures are from the Immigration and Refugee Board of Canada, Country Reports, 1998 to 2015 obtained upon request by the author. Czech figures appear in italic. All calculations by Cyntha Levine-Rasky (Queen's University) with the final graph made in consultation with Juliana Beaudoin.

few months later, the Conservatives won an absolute majority in the Canadian Parliament and used their power to revise many governmental regulations and structures – including the entire Canadian immigration and refugee system. The result was that in early 2012, Bill-C31, "Protecting Canada's Immigration System Act", was introduced.

In short, a two-tiered system was created for refugee applicants. Those applicants coming from countries that the Canadian government predetermined as "safe" [Designated Country of Origin (DCO)] were allotted a much shorter time to file for refugee status, their right to appeal was significantly curtailed and access to medical care severely reduced. As of October 2016, nearly all countries in the EU, including Hungary, are DCO. Although the Federal (2015) and Supreme Court (2016) has since struck down some of Bill C-31's provisions – all refugee claimants now have the right to appeal and to health care, regardless of country of origin – the political message was clear: the right to seek refuge was no longer safe for all refugee applicants. This change was reflected in the numbers. As of 2013, when Bill-C31 came into effect, Hungarian refugee approval rates fell from sixty to eighteen per cent in a matter of months and many awaiting appeal were deported back to Hungary.[10]

## Methods and materials

Recognising that media reflects power dynamics and politics reflects media (Fairclough 1995) we chose to analyse the co-constructive relationship across various media outlets. In order to analyse the predominant media discourse, we selected the largest daily newspapers in Hungary and Canada that also reflects the political diversity of the country: *Népszabadság* (NSZ) from the left-centre and *Magyar Nemzet* (MN) from the right-centre. As we discussed and concluded, these political divisions were much more prominent in Hungary (a phenomenon that Corneo (2005) coins "media capture"), than in Canada. Given that Canada is a bilingual (French/English) country, we strove to include the largest French-language paper, *La Presse,* in addition to the most circulated English-language press. The *Globe and Mail* is considered the "newspaper of record" covering major news events in the country. Politi-cally it would be considered centre-left. The *National Post* is typically con-sidered a more centre-right paper. Lastly we included the *Toronto Star* because it is widely read and we noted that many of the articles regarding Roma focused on the arrival and housing of Roma in Toronto, specifically. All of the newspapers have online and paper circulations between two and three million.

Particular time frames were selected reflecting the waves of Romani emigration as well as significant political and policy changes in both countries: 1999–2001, 2008–09 and 2011–13. In total there were 141 articles in 6 papers covering the particular issue of Roma from Hungary immigrating to Canada. There were some surprises – such as the dearth of coverage in 2008–09 compared to the other two periods – as well as significant changes in which newspapers covered the issue across the different time periods (Table 1). We note that in 1999–2001 *MN* only ran eight stories whereas *NSZ* published 29; by 2011–13 the numbers were almost completely reversed. As discussed later, perhaps such silence in Hungarian media may equate dissent.

We searched for themes, by creating "codes" to analyse both countries' papers.[11] Some of these codes – such as "judicial" or "The Economy" – were predetermined; others emerged as we began coding such as "Visa" and "Czech/Hungary comparison". Following Stake's (2006) suggestion, we coded all documents for each country separately and then engaged in a cross analysis. We were looking for themes, including patterns of difference.

**Table 1.** The number of articles in the analysed newspapers during the selected periods.

|  | Magyar Nemzet | Népszabadság | The Globe and Mail | Toronto Star | National Post | La Presse |
|---|---|---|---|---|---|---|
| 1999–2001 | 8 | 29 | 7 | 6 | 5 | 0 |
| 2008–09 | 6 | 4 | 1 | 5 | 0 | 1[a] (2010) |
| 2011–13 | 27 | 9 | 3 | 11 | 3 | 15 |
| *Sum* | *41* | *42* | *11* | *22* | *8* | *16* |

[a]Although there were no articles from 2008 to 2009, this 2010 piece is relevant to our discussion.

Some motives – such as "immigration policy" or "systemic racism" –  were evident in both. Some were particular to each case (i.e. "dehumanizing language" in the Canadian media or "double dipping for welfare" in Hungarian one) and did not "cross code".

As suggested by Hafner-Burton and Ron (2009) quantitative analysis allows one to see patterns of consistency and difference as well as track changes.

Qualitative analysis enables more in-depth analysis. When employing a mixed methods approach one can pinpoint where qualitative analysis can be most useful. In addition we coded the various actors in order to reveal the "role" that Roma played within the piece as well as their "worthiness" as simply victims rather than people with agency (Plaut 2012).

## Results

The Romani population in Canada is not particularly large, prominent or well-known thus at least half of the Canadian articles included some contextual background, of greater and lesser accuracy. Such background included the historical origins of Roma as well as mentioning how the transition from socialism had negative economic and social consequences for Roma in Central and Eastern Europe. In both English- and French-language papers it was presumed that the audience had little pre-existing knowledge. Although at times such background information came from Romani organizations and activists, often the source was not specifically referenced.

The majority of Roma from Hungary settled in two areas of Ontario: the Parkdale neighbourhood in Toronto and the city of Hamilton. This may explain why by 2001 the *Toronto Star* became the newspaper running the highest numbers of articles on the topic – the issue was not abstract, it was local news. In addition, certain journalists became the consistent voice covering the topic. These articles focused on how the community itself was adjusting and adapting to the large and rapid influx of Romani people. With the exception of two nuanced pieces about Parkdale schools[12] the tone of the articles was unquestionably positive towards Romani immigration. For example, there were two pieces highlighting Roma cultural festivals (from 2000 and 2012) as well as a photo exhibit pro-filing middle class Roma people in Canada and Europe. Although there was significant criticism about the overcrowding of accommodations and schools, this was portrayed as a failure of the municipal or federal government to provide adequate resources *not* a Roma specific problem. For example, the mayor of Hamilton describes the prevailing sentiment by local officials by saying:

> "Most of the Roma I know have jobs already; their biggest concern right now is for our Roma team to find a good soccer field". (Bigotry Keeps Roma on the Run; *Toronto Star*, November 6, 2011)

This differs greatly from the Hungarian newspapers. The emigration of Roma to Canada appears relatively rarely (only 1.91 per cent of all articles regarding Roma in both newspapers), coverage mainly discussed integration, discrimination, segregation or racism within Hungary. There was a sharp change between 2009 and 2011, when writing became more focused on the ethnicity of the people involved and radical discourses spread into mainstream (cf. Vidra and Fox 2012).[13]

There were two reasons given for Romani emigration: the search for better living conditions (most prevalent frame at the turn of the millennium) and racial discrimination (including violent racism and far-right movements which became much more prevalent beyond of the 2000s). Frames changed again in 2011–12, when a much more insidious discussion of Roma "taking advantage of welfare and social services" returned to the forefront in the analysed Hungarian press.

Although the Canadian press prides itself on in-depth and robust coverage of domestic and international issues, what is particularly noticeable in this case is the *lack* of diversity in perspectives: nearly all the articles agree that Roma are a specific ethnic group in Europe suffering from systematic discrimination and at times racially motivated violence. Nearly all agree that the treatment of Roma in Europe – and specifically in Hungary – is worsening. But only eight of the fifty-seven articles actually include reporting from Europe – six in Hungary one in Czech Republic and one in Romania. These long-form feature stories were written in 2009 and again in 2012 based on the aftermath of the serial killers in Hungary and the introduction of Bill-C31, respectively. The other ninety per cent of the articles all reported from a fairly narrow Canadian lens. They are focused on how *Canada,* and often specifically Toronto, is responding, or failing to respond, to this latest wave of refugees.

We engaged in a process of iterative and deductive coding. The five most common codes in the 141 pieces were: *immigration policy;* both *systemic racism* and *violent discrimination* tied as second; *bogus refugee; generosity within the welfare or social services system* (Figure 2). What is particularly noteworthy is that although the codes themselves are similar, what they mean within the different media-spheres differs greatly between the Hungarian and Canadian papers. Thus the *presence* of the terms does not speak to the framing.

Overwhelmingly the articles are focused on *immigration policy* and judicial matters in Canada (e.g. court cases reviewing immigration rulings or changes in the law itself) and in Hungary as well. Even when the articles are profiling a particular person or family, they are doing so in order to bring the details and debate regarding immigration policy to light for the audience. This was evident in the 1990s and continued throughout the entire time period in spite of significant political changes within Canada. For example the case of the "Botos Brothers" covered by the *Toronto Star* in 2000 and 2001 were

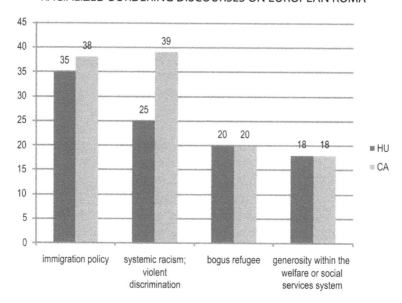

**Figure 2.** Most frequented codes in the Hungarian and Canadian newspapers.

clearly walking through the complicated immigration system with the story of well-known Hungarian Romani musicians. The same can be seen in a 2008 piece discussing the case of Adolf Horvath who, along with his wife and son, had been granted refugee status in Canada only to have it stripped because of questionable allegations of criminal activity in Hungary.[14] By illustrating what happened to the Horvath family, the article seemed to, once more, focus on problems of the politicization of the Canadian refugee system. It is assumed by both journalist and audience that the Canadian legal (and by extension, refugee) system should *not* be politicized and thus the treatment of Horvath (and by extension the Roma in general) is unusual and unacceptable.

In the Hungarian papers, nearly half of the articles addressing immigration focused on visa restrictions. The possible reinstatement of a visa for Hungary – which in the Hungarian press was assumed to be a reaction to the high number of Romani refugee applicants – was a very topical issue throughout all three time periods. Hungarian papers assumed that no one wanted to return to the days of needing a visa and both Hungarian and Canadian journalists made a continuous comparison between the imposition and lifting of the visa requirement for Czech and Hungarian nationals.

The comparison between Romani refugee applicants from the Czech Republic and Hungary as well as the governmental responses, was evident in many articles and this was not something that we were expecting. What is striking is that in the Hungarian papers the conflation of Czech/Hungarian Roma was based on this being a "Roma issue" whereas for Canada it was framed as an immigration policy issue.

In 1999, another dominant issue was the creation of a precedent made by the IRB, the so-called "lead cases". In the process, Hungarian representatives (including the leader of the National Roma Self-government) were invited to Canada to offer expert testimony. In *MN*, the story was framed as an independent, legal process made by an official Canadian body. On the other hand, *NSZ* questioned the independence of the  witnesses , accusing them of being "soldiers" for the Hungarian government.

"Lead cases" were seen as problematic in the Canadian press. By Roma being singled out as a distinct ethnic group in Canada rather than part of the "multicultural mosaic", they are portrayed as being *victims* of an incompetent and, at times racially biased, refugee system. Five articles specifically make mention of the problematic decision to use these "lead cases" to determine refugee claims from Romani asylum seekers.

In Canadian newspapers only seven cite too much **generosity** within the welfare or **social services system** – and one of those pieces is a letter to the editor. In *La Presse* there is one editorial which dealt with "The parasites", and two articles mentioned the economic consequence of Bill-C31 to the Canadian state budget discussing the "generosity" of the refugee system as problematic however these were the exceptions. Rather than Roma being the focus, articles framed the story around the inconsistency and presumed capriciousness of the system itself: are cases actually being determined on individual merit? (seven articles); is the system suffering from institutional bias? (eight articles); are immigration and refugee decisions being crafted for political reasons (six articles)? In these situations Roma become a prime example of a larger problem with the immigration system rather than a unique group of people with unique circumstances attempting to integrate into multicultural Canada.

As noted earlier, Bill-C31 was introduced on 16 February 2012 and after that nearly three quarters of the Canadian articles focused on that specific piece of legislation. Although the Hungarian press did cover Bill-C31, another story captured the majority of the limited Hungarian media attention: in January 2013 the Canadian government launched an unprecedented billboard campaign in Miskolc[15] which is home to a large Romani population. The goal of the billboards was to dissuade potential refugee claimants. This story was covered widely in the Hungarian press, emphasizing the political goal,[16] whilst it was barely mentioned on the Canadian side.

According to Levine-Rasky, Beaudoin, and St Clair (2014) and Beaudoin, Danch, and Rehaag (2015) there is a direct correlation between Bill-C31 and the international and domestic political rhetoric of the Canadian government (including the billboard campaign) resulting in both a drastic reduction of the number of refugee applicants from Hungary as well as the acceptance rate of those with pending refugee claims. Such interference was deemed "un-Canadian" by much of the Canadian press.

There was a shift in the way Hungarian papers framed "systemic racism". At the beginning of the analysed period, although acknowledging prejudice, the Hungarian papers were "cautious" in identifying racial discrimination or persecution.

> "Roma are really affected by discrimination, but it is not true that they are affected by racist persecution." –Kósáné Kovács Magdolna (chair of the committee of human, minority and religious rights in the Parliament. ("Kósáné: there won't be massive emigration" *NSZ*, January 9, 1999)

The right wing *MN* discussed the topic of racism only once in this period and did so in reporting on the facts of a particular legal case.

Starting in 2008, both the Hungarian and Canadian media addressed increases in violent racism by the Magyar Gárda and other organized vigilante groups throughout the country. When the topic emerges, the *violent racism* frame is the reason given for Roma migration to Canada.

> "Roma, with several hundred signed requests, asked the chair of National Gypsy Self-Government to help their emigration. They indicated serial attacks and discrimination as the reason for it." ("Hundreds of Gypsy are preparing for emigration" *NSZ*, August 26, 2009)

Hungarian-born Toronto writer Anna Porter wrote two in-depth feature pieces from Hungary published in the *Toronto Star*. They are some of the Canadian or Hungarian pieces to include interviews with "everyday" Hungarians. In her 2012 piece, Porter quotes Krisztina, an ethnic Hungarian mother:

> We are trying to protect our people and our culture ... They don't want to work. They should be taken away. We tried to integrate them. It didn't work. They should all go to Canada.

The article continues in Gyöngyöspata, where a serial killer was targeting Roma with police acquiescence,

> "We should put (the Roma) on a train and send them away" – Krisztina said, her 3 year old daughter running underfoot – (*Toronto Star*, October 13, 2012)

The few Canadian articles where Roma are mentioned as engaging in illegal activity – for example, selling false identification papers[17] or exaggerating claims of persecution[18] – were quick to point out that this was *not* a Roma specific problem but rather Roma were the latest example of an overall broken system. In fact, in all forty-one Canadian articles only two alluded to negative ethnically-based stereotypes of Roma when discussing Romani refugee applicants. With three exceptions, it was *never* assumed by the journalist that the main motivation for Roma coming to Hungary was to "take advantage" of Canada's economic resources. In fact, in the Canadian papers, the only time that "taking advantage of the welfare system/social benefits" was mentioned when quoting the Canadian government's position. This is very different to the Hungarian papers. At the end of the analysed periods, almost seventy per cent of the articles ended with a summary on Canadian benefits for refugees, thus insinuating that this is the motivation for Roma to migrate. Throughout 2012, in almost all the Canadian Roma related articles in *MN* used a common refrain: "each refugee costs 50,000 Canadian dollars for taxpayers". Although both Hungarian newspapers discussed and revealed that some Roma were collecting benefits from the Hungarian state while applying for refugee status in Canada ("double dipping") the rhetoric was much sharper in *MN*. Within five years the discursive framing/balance – in connection with migratory coverage – shifted significantly from racism to financial cunning.

The term of "bogus refugee" was first cited in the Canadian press in 2000 and eleven years later in the Hungarian newspapers. Except for an in-depth article in the *National Post* regarding the sale of forged papers, the term was only used in the Canadian press when quoting or making reference to the Canadian government's stances or accusations.[19] In Hungarian papers, around the millennium, narratives on "taking advantage" played a similar discursive role.

> "They arrived one after the other hoping for a chance at an effortless life, abusing generous services of local authorities during the refugee claim process." ("The rigour of democracy" *MN*, December 6, 2001)

However, by 2011 the term "bogus refugee" was being used quite regularly,[20] although there was a difference between the rhetoric of the two analysed newspapers. *NSZ* used softer terms such as "unauthorized",[21] or "unsubstantiated",[22] whilst *MN* applied stronger terms, such as *unfair,*[23] "fake refugee"[24] or "abuse" (in several cases) and ran headlines such as "Canada goes Hard" (*MN*, October 3, 2012) or "Thousands of 'Persecuted' Roma in Toronto: A Sympathetic Lawyer Descries Abused Welfare and Social Services" (*MN*, September 1, 2012). The term "bogus refugee" was consistently used in conjunction with the "abuse of social services/social welfare" frame thus painting an assumed correlation.

## Discussion

Our findings lead us to offer three contributions on the relationship between media, formal politics/policies and Roma. The role of media differs significantly in Hungary and Canada. As the centralization of both the political apparatuses and the media institutions increased in Hungary, our findings corroborate what Bajomi-Lázár (2013) and Corneo (2005) argue: the press increasingly served as a means of publicizing governmental policy. So how do media demonstrate *dissent*? As Fidesz grew in power, MN began publishing more pieces in support of their policies regarding Romani migration (twenty-seven pieces in 2011–13) and talked about "bogus refugee" and economic migration – NSZ on the other hand became increasingly silent (nine pieces during the same period); this is a direct reversal of what took place a decade previously. From the opposition position, in 1999–2001, NSZ operated with "discrimination" and the failed Roma policy of Fidesz as a reason for migration, whilst MN rarely (re)presented the issue with short (objective) news (only one op-ed in 2001) (eight pieces and twenty-nine, respectively). We argue this silence is partly the means of dissent within a highly centralized and politicized press. In Canada, however, the press envisions itself as the "4th estate" whose primary responsibility is to "watchdog" the policies of the government. As Strömbäck (2005) explains, the press actively engages in the democratic process but does so in different ways, in different political contexts. One of the ways that the press engages in democracy is by restraining those in power through intense scrutiny. Therefore as formal politics and policies became increasingly centralized in Canada, the press responded by increasing its *critical* coverage – this was particularly evident in *La Presse* and the *Toronto Star*.

According to communications scholars Hackett and Zhao (1998), journalism operates within and creates a "regime of objectivity" (passim). Objectivity requires dissent, but there are limits (Hallin 1994; Handley and Rutigliano 2012). Expanding on Hallin's notion of the "sphere of consensus", both Gladstone (2011) and Wade (2011) discuss how journalists both create and maintain this "consensus" in a rapidly shifting world. If an issue is a new issue, then there is vigorous debate and an attempt to hear and address both sides, but once something is within the "sphere of consensus" then a journalist can push and promote that perspective without even recognising that they are engaged in advocacy – they presume they are just reporting "the" (singular and unquestioned) truth (Zelizer 2004). Within the Canadian press, the benefits of multiculturalism are safely guarded within the sphere of consensus, thus the ethnic-specific reporting as found in some Hungarian papers (especially in *MN*) would be seen as inappropriate and indeed, a violation of "proper" journalism. Another assumed unquestioned truth is the non-politicisation of the refugee process in Canada. Thus when there appeared to be blatant state interference such as in three 1999 articles about lead cases as well as the "fact finding mission" in 2012, the Canadian media reacted negatively. The media was also suspicious if not critical when (then Citizen and Immigration Minister) Jason Kenney's publically made statements of "bogus refugees". Although politics always impacts immigration, the government was acting outside of the "sphere of consensus" by being so transparent and the media responded by publicizing such violations.

This is significantly different in the Hungarian press. As Vidra and Virág (2013) argued, besides the increasing deprivation, "the main driving force behind migration is ethnic discrimination and [failure to] accept this [reality] amounted to blaming the Roma for taking advantage of the refugee systems of other countries" (Vidra and Virág 2013, 156). The increasing politicalization of economic life shifted the sphere of consensus: Hungary is portrayed poorly in the international sphere, and Roma are part of the problem, but how this manifested in the articles differed between the two outlets. *NSZ* tried to show multiple sides of this complex sociological issue, whilst *MN* perpetuated negative stereotypes with terms such as "bogus refugee".

In analysing the texts itself, it became obvious that "the sphere of consensus", within these two media landscapes was vastly different, and this framed the limits of acceptable dissent within. In the Hungarian case it was assumed that readers would be familiar with particular negative stereotypes regarding Roma. On the other hand, in Canada, official multiculturalism makes the discussion of ethnicity, and particularly explanations of behaviour on the basis of ethnicity, a taboo subject within the media. It was also assumed that people would expect the newspapers to not take an explicitly partisan position; to do so would be violating the norms of journalism in Canada. We thus argue that Hallin's notion of the sphere of consensus, and Wade's recognition that this sphere is not stagnant but rather shifts, can be further refined by recognizing the importance of cultural and political contexts. Thus the same facts: Roma are migrating from Hungary to Canada and claiming refugee status becomes two different stories. We argue this is not only based on different norms of journalism practice (Mihelj 2011; Salovaara-Moring 2011) but that the socio-political discourses within the respective countries literally created different "facts".

One of the reasons that "Roma" become a different story is that "the Roma" are a discursive category itself – and one that differs, and changes, within the dynamic Hungarian and Canadian media. As discussed above, in Hungary the category "Roma" already comes with particular cultural associations and a conversation that is often highly politicized. For one, Roma and economic policies are deeply intertwined – whether the journalist or the reader agrees with said policies or not. In addition, the treatment of Roma is also connected to Hungarian international relations – in MN media Roma were often seen as an obstacle to good trade relations or travel (visa restrictions); in NSZ, the economic status of Roma as well as the racism, was often seen as a shame to Hungarian international reputation, particularly in the 1990s and early 2000s prior to EU accession.

This was very different from the Canadian media context where Roma were often portrayed as one more immigrant group and their integration spoke to the success of Canadian multiculturalism. In fact the majority of the articles about Roma in Canada are actually about Canada. Although the people in question were Roma, quite often the article was about the federal government's failure to uphold "Canadian values". Roma become a case study for a larger narrative of a broken, and increasingly politicized, Canadian immigration system.

## Conclusion

Our findings note a clear change in the "sphere of consensus" (Hallin 1994). More importantly, however, our findings note that this sphere of consensus was not static but rather a shifting co-constructed relationship with formal political realities (Wade 2011).

In sum, as noted throughout this article, whilst there was a clear distinction between the right- and left-wing papers in Hungary, there was almost none in the Canadian papers; hence the normal way of analysing media discourses of "right" and "left" does not work here in a cross comparison. Notwithstanding, the different politics and socio-cultural norms created vastly different "spheres of consensuses" within and between the Hungarian and Canadian papers. The framing is taking place *within* the changing political realities and priorities of the respective societies – thus although the "facts" appear to be the same, the stories are vastly distinct.

## Notes

1. More details in Kemény (2000).
2. Cf. Petrova (2004).
3. https://www12.statcan.gc.ca/nhs-enm/2011/as-sa/99-010-x/99-010-x2011001-eng.cfm#a2. Accessed June 21, 2016.
4. Mosaic Institute (2014) Perception and Reality of Imported Conflict in Canada. http://mosaicinstitute.ca/wp-content/uploads/2016/05/13.pdf Accessed June 21, 2016.
5. Canadian Council of Refugees datasheet (2016). http://ccrweb.ca/sites/ccrweb.ca/files/static-files/canadarefugeeshistory4.htm. Accessed June 21, 2016.
6. In 1997, Canada reinstated visa requirements for Czech nationals – this comparison between Roma from Czech Republic and Hungary was very evident in policy and media documents.
7. The 'lead case' was justified in providing 'guidance' but in practice it provided legitimation for curtailing acceptance of Romani applicants from Hungary. The Federal Court of Appeal ruled against the Lead Case in 2006. We thank one of the anonymous reviewers for insisting we clarify this point.
8. The decision to create and use lead cases was quite controversial and was eventually overturned in 2006.
9. *MN*, November 9, 2011.
10. According to statements made by current Canadian minister of immigration, as of October 2016, it appears that the DCO program may be eliminated by the end of 2016.
11. For complete list of the codes visit: http://www.regscience.hu:8080/jspui/bitstream/11155/1228/3/appendix_for_the_journal_article.pdf
12. Roma Children Perplex Local Educators; *Toronto Star*, November 28, 2009.
13. See more details in the 'Press discourses on Roma in the UK, Finland and Hungary' in this special issue.
14. As of June 2016 the case is, once again, under appeal.

15. Major city in Hungary, in one of the most economically depressed region, from where out-migration has been heaviest during the second wave (cf. Vidra and Virág 2013).
16. Both newspaper cited Zsolt Németh [state officer] who emphasised that ' … we avoided visa restriction'. *MN, May 24, 2013; NSZ, May 29, 2013.*
17. 'For Sale in Toronto: Fake Roma Papers' *National Post,* March 29, 2000.
18. 'Unbearable Lightness of Refugee Policy' *Toronto Star,* July 21, 2009.
19. *National Post,* March 29, 2000.
20. 'Human trafficking' *MN,* November 9, 2011.
21. 'Hot issues' *NSZ,* February 1, 2013.
22. e.g. *NSZ,* October 6, 2011.
23. 'Canada: Unfair refuge claims from Roma' *MN,* November 9, 2011.
24. 'Canada spends a lot on bogus refugee' *MN,* September 3, 2012.

## Acknowledgements

We thank to Dr Eric Spalding, who helped us locate the articles in *La Presse* thus ensuring that we could have a more comprehensive analysis of Canadian media landscape. We thank Gina Csanyi-Robah for offering her own reflections and perspectives as well as Professor Cynthia Levine-Rasky for sharing her graph and her consistent dedication through advocacy, scholarship and collegiality.

## Disclosure statement

No potential conflict of interest was reported by the authors.

## Funding

This work was supported by European Commission [grant number SSH.2011.4.2-1-290775] EUBORDERSCAPES project.

## References

Arhin, A. 2013. "Roma in Canada: Migratory Trends, Issues and Perceptions." In *Roma Migration to and from Canada,* edited by Zs. Vidra, 53–85. Budapest: CPS, CEU.
Baer, M., and A. Brysk. 2009. "New Rights for Private Wrongs: Female Genital Mutilation and Global Framing Dialogues." In *The International Struggle for New Human Rights,* edited by C. Bob, 14–29. Philadelphia: University of Pennsylvania Press.
Bajomi-Lázár, P. 2013. "The Party Colonisation of the Media: The Case of Hungary." *East European Politics & Societies* 27 (1): 69–89. doi:10.1177/0888325412465085.
Beaudoin, J., J. Danch, and S. Rehaag. 2015. "No Refuge: Hungarian Romani Refugee Claimants in Canada." *Osgoode Hall Law School Legal Studies Research Paper Series,* No.12. Accessed 27 April 2015. http://ssrn.com/abstract = 2588058.

Bernát, A. 2014. "Leszakadóban: a romák társadalmi helyzete a mai Magyarországon." [Lagging Behind: The Social Situation of Roma in the Recent Hungary]. In *Társadalmi Riport*, edited by T. Kolosi and I. Gy. Tóth, 246–264. Budapest: TÁRKI.

Bernáth, G., and V. Messing. 2013. *Pushed to the Edge. Research Report on the Representation of Roma Communities in the Hungarian Mainstream Media, 2011.* Budapest: CEU CPS.

Bodor, Á., Z. Grünhut, and R. Horeczki. 2014. "Socio-cultural Cleavages in Europe." *Regional Statistics* 4 (2): 106–125. doi:10.15196/RS04207.

Brown, P., P. Dweyer, and L. Scullion. 2013. *The Limits of Inclusion? Exploring the Views of Roma and Non Roma in Six European Union Member States: Final Research Report for the Roma SOURCE Project, 2.* Accessed 1 April 2014. http://www.romasource.eu/userfiles/attachments/pages/167/rs-finalresearchreport-full-2013-en.pdf.

Corneo, G. 2005. "Media Capture in a Democracy: The Role of Wealth Concentration." CESifo Working Paper, No. 1402.

Durst, J. 2002. "Innen az ember jobb, hogyha meg is szabadul. [It is better to leave here]." *Esély* 4: 99–121.

Durst, J. 2010. "'What Makes Us Gypsies, Who Knows … ?!': Ethnicity and Reproduction." In *Multi-disciplinary Approaches to Romany Studies*, edited by M. Stewart, and M. Rövid, 13–34. Budapest: CEU PRESS.

El-Nawawy, M., and A. Iskandar. 2002. "The Minotaur of 'Contextual Objectivity': War Coverage and the Pursuit of Accuracy with Appeal." *Transnational Broadcasting Studies* 9. Accessed 1 April 2014. http://www.tbsjournal.com/Archives/Fall02/Iskandar.html.

Engelhart, K. 2013. "Zjelko Jovanović on racism against Roma and what Roma want." *Macleans Magazine*, 31 October 2013. http://www.macleans.ca/general/on-racism-against-roma-and-how-it-varies-from-country-to-country-and-what-roma-want/ Accessed 14 January 2014.

Fairclough, N. 1995. *Media Discourse.* London: Edward Arnold.

Fraser, N. 1991. "Rethinking the Public Sphere: A Contribution to the Critique of Actually Existing Democracy." In *Habermas and the Public Sphere*, edited by C. Calhoun, 109–142. Cambridge, MA: MIT Press.

Fraser, A. 1995. *The Gypsies*, 2nd ed. Cambridge: Blackwell.

Gladstone, B. 2011. *The Influencing Machine: Brooke Gladstone on the Media.* New York: W.W. Norton and Company.

Gray, L. 2011. *First Nations 101.* Vancouver, BC: Adaawx.

Habermas, J. [1964]1974. "The Public Sphere: An Encyclopaedia Article." In *New German Critique, 3*, translated by S. Lennox and F. Lennox, 49–55.

Hackett, R. A., and Y. Zhao. 1998. *Sustaining Democracy: Journalism and the Politics of Objectivity.* Toronto: Garamond Press.

Hafner-Burton, E., and J. Ron. 2009. "Seeing Double: Human Rights Impact Through Qualitative and Quantitative Eyes." *World Politics* 61 (2): 360–401.

Hallin, D. 1994. *We Keep America on Top of the World: Television Journalism and the Public Sphere.* New York: Routledge.

Handley, R., and L. Rutigliano. 2012. "Journalistic Field Wars: Defending and Attacking the National Narrative in a Diversifying Journalistic Field." *Media Culture Society* 34: 744–760. doi:10.1177/0163443712449500.

Kemény, I. 2000. "The Structure of Hungarian Roma Groups in Light of Linguistic Changes." *REGIO* 1: 105–116.

Kemény, I. 2005. *Roma of Hungary. East European Monographs.* New York, NJ: Atlantic Research and Publications.

Kováts, A., ed. 2002. *Roma Migration*. Budapest: HAS IMR.

Kymlicka, W. 1995. *Multicultural Citizenship*. Oxford: Oxford University Press.

Levine-Rasky, C., J. Beaudoin, and P. St Clair. 2014. "The Exclusion of Roma Claimants in Canadian Refugee Policy." *Patterns of Prejudice* 48 (1): 67–93.

Mihelj, S. 2011. *Media Nations: Communication Belonging and Exclusion in the Modern World*. London: Palgrave MacMillian.

Open Society Foundation. 2010. *No Data – No Progress: Data Collection in Countries Participating in the Decade of Roma Inclusion 2005–2015*. New York: Open Society Foundation.

PER (Project on Ethnic Relations). 2000. *Roma and Statistics*. Report on the Roma and Statistics roundtable, Strasbourg, France.

Petrova, D. 2004. *The Roma: Between a Myth and the Future*. European Roma Rights Centre. Accessed 16 February 2012. http://www.errc.org/cikk.php?cikk = 1844.

Plaut, S. 2012. "Expelling the Victim by Demanding Voice: The Counterframing of Transnational Romani Activism." *Alternatives: Global, Local, Political* 37 (1): 52–65.

Pusca, A. 2012. *Eastern European Roma in the EU: Mobility, Discrimination, Solutions*. New York: Idebate Press.

Salovaara-Moring, I. 2011. "What is Europe? Geographies of Journalism." In *Media, Nationalism and European Identities*, edited by M Sokosd, and K. Jakubowicz, 49–71. Budapest: CEU Press.

Stake, R. 2006. *Multiple Case Study Analysis*. New York: Guilford Press.

Stewart, M. 1997. *In the Time of the Gypsies*. Boulder, Colorado: Westview Press.

Strömbäck, J. 2005. "In Search of a Standard: Four Models of Democracy and Their Normative Implications for Journalism." *Journalism Studies* 6 (3): 331–345.

Thelen, P. 2005. *Roma in Europe: From Social Exclusion to Active Participation*. Skopje, Macedonia: Friedrich Ebert Stiftung.

UNDP. 2003. *Avoiding the Dependency Trap: The Roma Human Development Report*. Accessed 10 January 2012. http://hdr.undp.org/en/reports/regional/europethecis/name,3203,en.html.

UNDP. 2011. *Beyond Transition: Toward Inclusive Societies*. Bratislava, Slovakia: United Nations Development Programme/Regional Bureau for Europe and the Commonwealth of Independent States.

Vidra, Zs., ed. 2013. *Roma Migration to and from Canada*. Budapest: CEU CPS.

Vidra, Zs. 2014. "Introduction." In *Facing the Far-right: Ethnographic Portrayals of Local Civil Resistance*, edited by Zs. Vidra, 5–23. Budapest: CEU CPS.

Vidra, Zs., and J. Fox. 2012. *The Radicalization of Media Discourse. The Rise of the Extreme Right in Hungary and the Roma Question*. Budapest: CEU CPS.

Vidra Zs., and T. Virág. 2013. "Some Hypotheses and Questions on the New Wave of Hungarian Roma Migration to and from Canada." In *Roma Migration to and from Canada*, edited by Zs. Vidra, 129–162. Budapest: CEU CPS.

Wade, L. 2011. "Journalism, Advocacy and the Social Construction of Consensus." *Media, Culture and Society* 33: 1166–1185. doi:10.1177/0163443711418273

Zelizer, B. 2004. "When Facts, Truth, and Reality are God-terms: On Journalism's Uneasy Place in Cultural Studies." *Communication and Critical/Cultural Studies* 1 (1): 100–119.

# Coping with everyday bordering: Roma migrants and gatekeepers in Helsinki

Miika Tervonen and Anca Enache

**ABSTRACT**

The article analyses intra-European bordering on the local level through the case of Eastern European Roma in Helsinki. Precarious EU migrants outside the Nordic labour markets have formed a group neither "in" nor completely "out" of national welfare structures. We argue that various level authorities have responded to the loss of direct control over legitimate yet unwanted migrants by mobilizing municipal workers and local police as everyday gatekeepers. Policy towards the Roma migrants in Helsinki is ethnicized (conceptualizing them as a special category requiring targeted measures) and "NGOized" (relegating elementary social provision to the third sector). Their presence of is not formally challenged, yet they are effectively without access to social rights and pathways to permanent residence. Meanwhile, the migrants strive to improve their disadvantaged position through transnational, family-based livelihood strategies, which are actively adapted to the shifting European and Finnish borderscapes.

## Introduction

In the last three decades, there has been a consistent drive in the Nordic countries towards a more restrictive and selective immigration policies (e.g. Brochmann and Hagelund 2011). However, this trend has been contradicted by the membership in the EU free movement regime. Finland and other Nordic countries have thus been connected to a passport-free area with more than 400 million residents. These include millions of Eastern and Central European Roma, many of whom have experienced deepening margin-alization and discrimination at the same time as border crossings have become easier. Roma communities have consequently experienced dispro-portionately high rates of emigration after the collapse of the socialist regime, intermediated through agency, networks and varying resources (cf. Vlase and Voicu 2013).

In the receiving Western European countries as well as in Canada, the media and political debates have frequently framed the mobility of the Eastern European Roma as a threat to public safety and welfare, and as one of the issues questioning the legitimacy of the EU free mobility principle (Sigona and Trehan 2009; Nacu 2011). The migrants have been constructed through racialized and exoticizing discourses, separating them from "normal" migration issues (Benedik 2010; Grill 2012; Van Baar 2014) and legitimizing targeted restrictive policies (Nacu 2011; Sigona 2011). Aside from the highly publicized expulsions by Italian and French authorities, borderline legal measures in curbing Westward migration of Roma have been documented throughout Europe (Bigo, Carrera, and Guild 2013).

In the present article, we examine the situation of the Eastern European migrants of primarily Roma ethnicity in Helsinki in order to analyse the politics of intra-European borders on the local level. We examine interaction between local gatekeepers (Iacovetta 2006), NGO actors and the migrants. How do the increasingly selective and securitized European migration regimes deal with migrants who are nominally legitimate yet perceived as undesirable? Favell (2014) argues that freedom of movement of persons has been largely beneficial for most intra-European migrants. But what kind of opportunities and risks has it meant for precarious migrants at the margins of affluent host societies?

The article contributes to the growing literature on the mobilities of diverse Roma populations within Europe (Grill 2011; Vitale and Legros 2011; Picker 2013) and beyond (Bigo, Carrera, and Guild 2013). This research has deconstructed stereotypes of "nomadic" Roma cultures, highlighting diverse logics of mobility, the agency of the migrants in improving their disadvantaged living condition, and the violent impact of nationalism and neoliberal reforms (Sigona and Trehan 2009; Bunescu 2014; Manzoni 2016). Also in Nordic countries, successive media frenzies have been followed by a gradual growth of research literature (e.g. Enache 2012; Markkanen 2012; Tervonen 2012; Engebrigtsen 2014; Roman 2014; Djuve et al. 2015; Jokela 2016).

However, mainstream debates on migration still frequently bypass Romani mobilities as separate or marginal case, reproducing a "splendid isolation" of the traditional Romani studies (Willems 1998). For us, the case of the Roma migrants in Helsinki offers a possibility to study core challenges in contemporary social citizenship and rebordering in Europe (Van Baar 2014). The Roma migrants can be seen as a part of a growing diversity of migrants with "in-between" statuses, facing a multitude of gatekeepers in their everyday dealings with health care centres, schools, workplaces, banks, etc. As argued by Mezzadra and Neilson (2013), management of migration increasingly functions through the regulation of migrants' access to permanent residence and social and economic rights. At the same time, there has been a reactivation across Europe of legislation and policies resembling earlier vagrancy laws, in an attempt to stem a "free movement of poverty" in general, and the mobility of racialized Roma migrants in particular (Fekete 2014).

We examine these developments in the case of Helsinki through an approach that is inspired by Yuval-Davis's focus on micro-scale everyday bordering practices in order to understand changing European borders (Yuval-Davis 2013, 16). The article is based primarily on interviews and fieldwork conducted 2014–16 in the Helsinki metropolitan area. We have conducted participant observation and completed seventeen in-depth semi-structured interviews in Helsinki with Romanian Roma migrants, social workers, police, activists and NGO representatives. Municipal and government policy documents, NGO materials and newspaper discourses have also been analysed.[1]

It is important to note that what we refer to here as "Eastern European Roma migrants" is not one bounded group with shared features and identity, but comprises individuals and families whose migration experiences vary fundamentally according to socio-economic context, age, gender, religion, family status, language skills and health. While the migrants we interviewed mostly self-identify as "Roma", many resist the hegemonic discourse that lumps all Romanian and Bulgarian street workers into one group, and stress the difference between various groups and nationalities. Labelling someone as a "Gypsy" ("Tigan") is in fact often used in negative sense in order to distinguish between acceptable and shameful behaviour: "what can you expect from them? He, who is a Gypsy in Romania, is a Gypsy here, too (male interviewee, 45 years)".

## Responding to unwanted EU migrants: a "policy of no policy"

After the EU's eastward expansion in 2007, small groups of Romanian and Bulgarian Roma migrants began arriving to Finland and other Nordic countries.[2] Despite seemingly insignificant numbers – with estimates of yearly visitors varying in Finland between 300 and 500 persons before 2016 – the migrants became subjects of public outcry verging on moral panic. Following a European pattern (e.g. Benedik 2010), they were framed as an ethnically distinctive and fundamentally problematic special case, the "Roma beggars".

There is a historical continuity in treating migrants labelled as "Gypsies" as automatically suspicious (Lucassen 1997), with targeted restrictions in force in Nordic countries up until the 1950s (Tervonen 2016). However, there are also contemporary factors making the issue sensitive in the Nordic countries. As Djuve, Friberg, Tyldum and Zhang argue (2015, 9–10), these countries "have a long tradition of strict regulation of entry and residence on one hand, and generous welfare arrangements and redistribution of income among their own citizens and other legal residents on the other". EU citizens who were at the same time visibly poor and homeless, and lacked permanent residency, and thus access to national social security, appeared as deeply anomalous to notions of universal Nordic welfare state (Lindström 2015, 37–37).

While inclusive welfare policies have appeared as institutionally problematic and politically unrealistic, the free movement regulations meant that the migrants could not be simply be kept out, either. An implicit policy dilemma has thus emerged, underlying a plethora of committee memoranda, reports and policy debates: how to deter Roma migrants from coming into Finland, in spite of their right to do so? This dilemma is visible in a number of control-oriented initiatives: proposals for criminalizing begging and "low-quality musical performances" (parliamentary debates from 2008 onwards; initiatives by ministry of interior in 2010 and by conservative MPs in 2016); a ban on illicit camping; legislative proposals against human trafficking and "organizing begging" (2010); and setting up a special register on beggars (2014).

By 2016, however, none of these initiatives had led to significant legislative changes. Meanwhile, there were few serious debates on inclusive social policy responses. In official memoranda and reports, the range of positive policies presented as possible is extremely limited, bearing resemblance to what Vitale (2008) has called the reduction of local policy instruments in relation to Roma and Sinti in Italy. Neither of two national committees dealing with the position of the Roma migrants in Finland in 2009–2010 could suggest concrete positive measures in addition to proposed restrictions. A major attempt in 2015 to expand the health care of so-called paperless migrants would have explicitly excluded the EU migrants had it passed, actually worsening the possibilities of most Roma migrants to access health services.[3]

As Djuve et al. (2015, 9–10) argue in the Scandinavian context, both those working on a policy goal of "keeping them out" as well as those who wish to "alleviate their situation" find themselves with a very limited scope for policy-making in relation to the street-working EU migrants. What has emerged is a kind of a "policy of no policy". The Finnish central government and ministries have been unable or unwilling to take active stance or to formulate explicit public policy towards legal residents who are visibly not meeting the basic social rights that the Finnish welfare state is committed into maintaining. The lack of clear policy or guidelines from the central government has left the issue largely to local authorities, particularly in Helsinki, where the majority of the migrants have arrived.

### City of Helsinki: gatekeeping and ambivalence

The Finnish state's inability to formulate explicit policy on the destitute situation of the Roma migrants has been mirrored on the local level in the City of Helsinki. In 2011, for example, a long-standing city committee considering alternatives to illegal camping of the Roma concluded that it cannot present any viable alternative solutions (City of Helsinki 2011). Besides constraints imposed by the EU and national legislation, a scarcity of positive policy tools is connected to a fear of providing "incentives" for further migration. This worry recurs in policy documents and memoranda, with the police expressing anxiety about "our country's attractiveness in the eyes of the Roma beggars" (City of Helsinki 2011, 27), or the responsible social official justifying the city's unwillingness to offer accommodation or health services by stating that "we do not want to encourage the begging phenomenon" (Jarmo Räihä in *Helsingin Sanomat*, January 9, 2009).

Yet, the absence of explicit policies has not mean passivity of the city authorities. On the contrary, we argue that the city of Helsinki authorities have sought to deter migration by innovating indirect bordering techniques.[4]

Externally, the diverse Helsinki city authorities have sought to track and reduce migration by cooperating with authorities and local communities in the sending regions, particularly in rural Romania. The police and social authorities have formed a contact with their Romanian counterparts, and several delegations of the City officials travelled to Romania. A practice has been developed of inviting Romanian police to Finland to help local police in gathering information and communicating with the migrants.

The most important response, however, seems to have been a mobilizing of executive municipal officials as *de facto* gatekeepers in Helsinki. In 2010, the City mayor thus set up a so-called "Roma working group" (*romanityöryhmä*, also known as the "working group on begging"), which was tasked with coordinating between different city departments in order to "reduce and prevent the negative by-products of the begging" (City of Helsinki 2011, 3). A key policy towards this goal became a tough line on "illegal" camping. Systematic evictions and demolitions of temporary camp sites and squats were carried out by the police and the Public Works Department, prompted by requests by the City of Helsinki. Between 2008 and 2011, this pitted the city authorities against activists who were providing shelter for Roma migrants in squatted houses and in the autonomous social centres. A highly publicized struggle between the city and the activists and migrants culminated as the city leadership co-opted or mobilized in turn the Social board, Environmental centre, Public Works Department, Real Estate Department, Youth Department, Rescue department and finally in 2011 the police (that provided executive assistance with a riot team wearing commando masks) in shutting down the social centre in Kalasatama, evicting a camp with between thirty and fifty residents (Jokela 2016).

Subsequently, the overwhelming majority of Roma migrants in Helsinki have slept rough in parks, woods, abandoned buildings or cars, all of which are illegal camping places according to the regulations of the municipality. In a game of hide-and seek, the police and Public Works Department have routinely handed eviction notices to migrants in temporary camp sites, clearing them with police backup, after which the homeless migrants simply move to another location.

Meanwhile, legal places to sleep are either too expensive for the migrants, or, in the case of the municipal public shelters, restricted to residents. As EU citizens are entitled to "emergency support" in the host country, defining what social rights this actually entitles to has become a contentious issue (Lindström 2015, 5–6). Before 2016, the city authorities adopted a position of denying any obligation to offer emergency accommodation to the Roma migrants, and issued guidelines explicitly excluding non-residents from such housing.

The legality of the policy has subsequently been called into question by activists and member of the city council members. For grassroots-level social workers, however, the situation remains unclear. As a senior social worker argues, they confront potentially life-threatening situations of the migrants, while working under ambiguous and possibly even illegal instructions:

> Of course we have real disputes about this within the bureau. [...] The line of the bureau [towards giving emergency housing to the Roma migrants] is: no, no no and no. But any of us can be the one who's there [on duty at the social emergency service] and its minus 25 degrees Celsius and there is no accommodation to offer. And if someone then freezes to death there on our backyard, the one held responsible is not the Deputy mayor, but the individual [social] worker out there.

Another area in which social workers have assumed a contentious role of gatekeepers has been the policy towards minor children and youth. From 2008 onwards, a policy was actively communicated to the Roma migrants, using for example leaflets printed in Romanian and Bulgarian, that the child protection officials would take any underage persons into custody if they were found begging or in improper housing and living conditions. While a senior social worker claims that this amounted to a conscious "scaremongering tactic", it was evidently successful in that minors largely stopped accompanying their parents into Finland.[5]

Aside from social workers, our interviews pointed to groups such as health care professionals, environmental workers and police facing legal and moral ambivalence in their engagements with the Roma migrants. Among the police, there have been also public expressions of wariness over the use of resources in maintaining what appeared as a self-perpetuating cycle of evicting migrant campsites (e.g. *Yle Helsinki* 14 June 2011). A senior constable admitted to us that he considers the recurrent evictions potentially counterproductive, but defended the practice by referring to the maintenance of public order and societal norms:

This question is highly problematic. We know that they will look for another place to camp. But this is how it goes. And we have had bad experiences from previous long-term camps [in Rajasaari and Kalasatama], which reflected negatively on their environments and were insecure for the inhabitants themselves. It's also a phenomenon that does not fit in with the Finnish society or culture.

Overall, the indirect everyday bordering in Helsinki shifts the burden of interpreting unclear social rights of the homeless EU migrants from policy-makers to the street-level police and municipal workers. Meanwhile, the provision of some of the elementary social welfare has been relegated over to third sector actors.

### Ngo patches in a policy void: the case of Hirundo

Mirroring an "NGOization" of the human rights of Roma minorities in Eastern Europe, there has been in a Western Europe a tendency to fund NGOs, charities and foundations in order to provide rudimentary services for Roma migrants, rather than extending normal welfare provisions (Trehan 2009). The City of Helsinki has followed this pattern. Since 2010, acute social services for homeless EU migrants have been predominantly provided by the *Hirundo* drop-in centre, funded in large part by the City of Helsinki, and run by the Helsinki Deaconess Institute (Puurunen, Enache, and Markkanen 2016).

In 2011, the City and the Helsinki Deaconess Institute opened the *Hirundo* drop-in centre in order to provide acute social support for Roma migrants. The centre was an outcome of a previous project *Rom pod rom,* that had been tasked with providing acute support and exploring possibilities to facilitate the migrants' return to home countries (Helsinki Deaconess Institute 2010; Leinonen and Vesalainen 2008, 7). After the eviction of the *Kalasatama* social centre, *Hirundo* became a central point for the Roma migrants. It provides a space in which to take care of basic hygienic needs, have coffee and rest during the daytime. The centre has showers, laundry, food warming facilities and sofas. As most of the migrants sleep rough, these facilities are intensively used. The names that the migrants call the centre reflects its functions: it is commonly called "the shower", or "the social". The latter refers to *Hirundo's* role as a transnational knot in migratory trajectories, a place where migrants exchange information on transportation and street work, charge phones, call home and store their belongings.

Another function of the centre's staff is to facilitate the migrants' interaction with authorities. *Hirundo* has also became an interface with a multiplicity of NGO and third sector actors. Volunteers from religious, political and health-related NGOs and networks, a street vending magazine "*Iso numero*" ("Big Issue"), researchers, journalists, artists, neighbours, employers and voluntary hosts reach out to the migrants though the centre

(Puurunen, Enache, and Markkanen 2016). Shifting cooperative relations and alliances emerged between the centre, the diverse actors and the migrants.

However, the centre is not mandated nor has the resources to tackle either of the two main problems which the migrants face: the lack of work and housing. In late afternoons, the migrants thus have to leave and find shelter outdoors, even in freezing winter nights. A worker of Hirundo told us that in relation to its homelessness users, the centre's service thus has the character of a "band aid": "We put a plaster on a wound but the wound itself does not heal". Another worker points to the powerlessness felt when appearing as semi-official advocate for migrants, whose social rights the counter-level municipal workers frequently seek to deny:

> Someone has a terrible toothache and you take her to the hospital. Once there, a real fight begins, with hostility and negative attitudes towards you as someone who brought an unwanted person there, and towards the potential patient herself. "Does she have a European Health Insurance Card? Or an insurance? Address? Money to pay for the invoice?" Meanwhile, you as a translator and an advocate have to tailor the right answers that would provide the wanted result: an appointment with a dentist.

Through its daily workings, the *Hirundo* centre provides concrete aid to migrants largely outside normal welfare provision. However, the centre and its workers are situated in a tense institutional space between the city of Helsinki, its counter-level workers, activists and the migrants themselves, and lack resources to alter the situation of the latter. Meanwhile, through legitimizing its funding through ethnicized "misery discourses" (Vesterberg 2016) the centre participates in the knowledge production over the migrants, self-reinforcing a conceptualization of the Eastern European Roma as a "vulnerable" category in need of special measures. The case of *Hirundo* thus highlights dilemmas of NGOized and "ethnified" social provision, as well as the underlying contradictions between the inclusive and exclusive strains in the policy of the City of Helsinki.

## Migrants' perspective: improving lives in the margins of Finnish borderscapes

Despite diverse backgrounds and resources, the lives of the migrants we interviewed in Helsinki are structured by a shared set of basic opportunities, constraints and risks. In contrast to many other "irregular" migrants, "deportability" (De Genova 2002) was not an issue for them. The migrants had experienced little if any oversight when entering Finland, or in regards to the obligation of register their stay with the police after three months' stay in the country.[6]

However, being overwhelmingly outside the regular labour market means that most migrants have little chance for long-term stay, not to mention permanent residence, in Finland. Most have worked in Romania mainly in the informal economy, as day labourers for private farms owners, cleaners for the municipality, or selling products such as second-hand clothes. In Finland, they have little access to the highly regulated labour market, and mostly consider finding work unrealistic. Instead, they seek to generate income through diverse informal economic activities. But being outside the regular labour market affects all areas of life in Finland, feeding into the lack of housing, healthcare and education, and exposing the migrants to multiple obstacles in their dealings with the police, social and health care workers, private security guards, etc.

Yet, the migrants we spoke with kept coming back to Finland from year to year. Indeed, it was apparent that many had managed to turn visits in Finland into a source of tangible and collective life improvement. "Ioana", for example, a former agricultural worker and a mother of five, has visited Finland on nine successive years together with her husband. For her, the logic of visiting Finland is straightforward:

> We came to Finland because there was no work. The borders opened and we had to leave to be able to raise our children. [In Romania] we struggle to live. I don't have a house. We live at my mother-in-law's house, with ten other families. [...] Here at least we have a chance to do something. We're earning money and sending it back home.

Below, we examine the strategies and the agency that the migrants such as Ioana employ in Helsinki, in coping with everyday risks and improving their lives; as well as the adaptations to the Finnish borderscapes this involves.

On one fundamental level, adaptations to the bordering and the opportunities in Helsinki begins already in the selection of who undertakes the expensive journey there. The strict child protection policy means that underage children and youth have been almost completely absent. At the same time, the possibility to beg without directly breaking the law seems to enable the circular migration of people in particularly precarious positions in their home countries, including women and the elderly. In its social composition, the population of street-working migrants in Helsinki thus resembles closely that found in a comparative study of Djuve et al. in Stockholm: large, relatively traditional and economically marginal Roma kin groups, including roughly similar numbers of women and men are prominent. This contrasts markedly with the picture of Copenhagen, for example, where a strict policy of enforcing a begging ban has led to the predominance of more mobile and less outwardly conspicuous single men among the streets workers (Djuve et al. 2015).

For those who *have* arrived, our interviews and ethnographic observations point to risk-reducing strategies well-documented among diverse populations living with highly insecure livelihoods (e.g. Portes, Castells, and Benton 1989; Fontaine and Schlumbohm 2000). Among these are the diversification and multi-locality of economic activities; the tapping of both informal and formal sources of income; and the sharing risks and resources within the context of families and kin networks. As particular migrants families become regular visitors to Helsinki, they also begin to acquire denser networks of local hosts, helpers, clients and employers, and to accumulate knowledge of the physical and institutional environment in Helsinki.

### Adaptive family economies

The main preoccupation of the migrants we talked to in Helsinki was to generate income while in Finland. The most important of the informal street work activities are the selling *Iso Numero* magazine ("Big Issue"), begging and collecting bottles. It is clear that income from each of these activities alone is very low and insecure. This income also has to cover travel costs and living expenses in Finland. Only after that can money be saved for specific goals, from keeping children in school to paying medical bills to fixing a leaking roof.

Competition poses a challenge. Increasing numbers of people arrive each year to compete for the limited income available through street work. We frequently heard complaints of lessening income from begging and selling street magazines, and of too many people collecting bottles. In general, there is a fear that Helsinki residents are "tired of giving money" (female interviewee, 28 years).

Yet, despite competition and low income from each individual activity, our informants frequently manage to earn enough not only to cover living and travel costs, but also to send remittances home. Achieving this is far from a trivial challenge, and seems to connect to an "adaptive family economy" (Fontaine and Schlumbohm 2000, 3), in which multiple economic activities are flexibly combined with each other, with the members of a particular family network being active in a variety of fields in order to tap a diversity of income sources.

Accordingly, none of the activities outlined above were the *only* sources of income for the migrants we interviewed. The so-called "beggars" also sell *Iso numero* magazine, collect bottles and tap seasonal earning possibilities such as selling flowers or berries. There is busking, selling of scrap metal, posing as human statues and selling of small items, postcards, etc. And whenever it is possible, income in street work is supplemented or substituted with paid work.

This diversity of economic activities recurs in our interviews, and has also been documented by Djuve et al in Scandinavian capitals (Djuve et al. 2015,

55). In cases in which an interviewee named only one income-generating activity, they practiced these in the context of a family economy in which also other activities were used. The case of "Ona" illustrates the functional division of work and income within a family:

> Ona sells *Iso numero* every day at the central railway station, staying in a relatively quiet spot with less competition. Her husband, Claudiu, collects cans around the city and looks for potential places to sleep in. Claudiu buys food for both of them with his share of the income. Meanwhile, Ona's earnings are used to buy phone cards, with which the couple stays in touch with their three children in Romania. Ona is determined to save at least 5€ of her earnings every day, in order to send money to the grandparents taking care of their children. Ona shows us a calling card of an international money-wiring service, which is worn out in continuous use. (Fieldwork diary, Tervonen)

In a gendered division of economic roles, Claudiu engages in more mobile activities, while Ona earns money through begging and selling the *Iso numero* magazine, which are more stationary and depend on evoking sympathy in the passersby. Ona is in fact the main earner of the family. But while collecting bottles brings only limited income (Djuve et al. 2015), it serves also other functions. Finding a shelter is a daily challenge that is made more acute by the city authorities' attempts to root out illicit camping. The constant risk of eviction from any particular campsite makes is important for to have multiple options available. As many other migrant men, Claudiu thus went around parks, woods and abandoned buildings in the daytime, in order not only to collect bottles but also to locate potential campsites. Information is shared within kin groups, which also seek to sleep in the same place for increased physical safety.

Our interviewees generally felt the presence of family and kin in Helsinki as a crucial safety net in the face of a highly insecure environment. The overwhelming majority had travelled to Helsinki with one or several close family members as well as members from the same extended kin group. They had also made the decision to come to Finland based on information from relatives who had previously visited the country.

While children usually remain at the home country, supporting them and paying for their school fees is frequently given as the main reasons for coming to Finland. Most of our interviewees send money home whenever they can, and use a significant share of their income to communicate with their children and relatives. Many practice a rotation (Näre 2011; Enache 2013), in which some of the adult family members – spouses, adult children and grandparents for example – stay in the home country, taking care of the dependent children. Meanwhile, other extended family members are engaged in income-generating activities not in one but in several Western European countries.

With 28 year old "Adrian", for example, his father was at the time of the interview employed at a construction site in Italy; his sister was doing agricultural work in Portugal; and his brother collecting bottles and recycling second-hand clothes in Norway. Adrian's mother, meanwhile, is one of the handful of Romanian Roma who has found salaried employment in Finland, combining two part-time jobs. Adrian himself has been working in short-term construction jobs in Italy and Spain. He had recently arrived to Finland, and was in the exceptionally good position of selling the *Iso numero* magazine and looking for work while living at his mother's hired apartment.

The migration diversifies the economic activities of the extended families, and results in the families' and extended family groups' livelihoods taking on a multi-local dimension, in which remittances and transnational exchange of information have a central importance (Markkanen 2012; Enache 2013).

### *Networking and sharing information*

Building bridging ties with local "good helpers" (Engebrigtsen 2014) is crucially important for many of the Roma migrants we interviewed in Helsinki. The former include regular givers of money, food and clothes, as well as hosts, employers, activists, journalists and other useful connections. The migrants actively acquire and share information about such helpers, as well as of the physical and institutional environment in Helsinki. Our fieldwork points to a significant potential payoff for those who manage to establish connections with regular helpers.

This is clear in relation to finding paid work. A handful of migrants have each year been able to find temporary employment with help from various civil society and NGO actors, as well as private helpers.[7] Also in finding accommodations the migrants can gain much by connecting with private and civil society actors. Many have been provided temporary shelter over the years by activists. Private people providing temporary housing have also become important. Among the hosts, Pentecostals and Finnish Roma appear as particularly prominent. Not all housing providers are motivated by philanthropism: some of our informants hire private rooms from acquaintances.

The way begging is practiced in Helsinki reflects the importance of relationships with particular helpers, competition with other street workers, and adaptations to everyday bordering. All of these combine to make the practice of begging in Helsinki highly stationary: the same people sit in the same place day by day, seeking to return to same spot each time they are in Finland. This is partly necessitated by the city policy: asking for money is allowed in Helsinki, but only as long as it is practiced "passively", that is, sitting down. Otherwise it is considered as "aggressive" and mandates police intervention. However, the stationary nature of begging has also economic upside. Our interviewees told us that if someone sat in the same place for a longer time, they begin to form relationships with "regulars". This is important, since a small core group of donors can provide the bulk of the daily income, while "most people give nothing" (as told by "Dariana", 26 years and "Loredana", 33 years). As the net income from begging is frequently very low, even one person giving more money than the usual 1–2€ can make a difference to daily earnings.

As relationships develop with regular helpers, these sometimes offer food, clothes or even accommodation. The regulars are seen as so valuable that they merit daily trips to distant suburbs with relatively few potential donors. "Elvira", for example, takes a train every day to sit at the same shopping centre in a suburb some 10 km from the centre of Helsinki. The place is familiar to her as her mother was previously given long-term accommodation there by a Pentecostal Finnish Roma woman. Elvira has visited the shopping centre for several years, but told us that she had earned little lately, as her regular helpers are away for the summer holidays.

As in Elvira's "inheriting" a regular begging spot from her mother, sharing local information seems crucial for our interviewees. Everything from finding abandoned houses to accessing a doctor depends on it. Activities such as collecting bottles also require knowledge of the urban environment and outdoors events. Many of the migrants we met were strikingly well informed of public events around the city.

Together with the adaptive family economies, the networks formed in Helsinki seem to provide the migrant street workers in Helsinki with enough everyday reliability to make the recurring trips to Finland feasible and, in most cases, also economically worthwhile. This does not mean that everyday life in Helsinki is not for most migrants harsh, at times apparently almost excruciating, involving a multitude of serious risks. The constant fear of evictions forces many migrants into a severe daily schedule, in which the makeshift shelters in forests or abandoned buildings are entered at late at night and exited early in order to avoid being spotted. Some of our interviewee's trips to Helsinki were stopped by acute health problems or accidents, as they could not access necessary medical treatment in Finland.

Despite frequent experiences of hardship, the coping strategies of the interviewees mean that many of them are able to turn the economically and physically insecure environment in Helsinki into a source of collective livelihood improvement. A middle-aged couple "Costa" and "Maria", for example, credited the buying of a house in Romania largely to the income they had pieced together in Finland, and presented this as a great triumph for their family. Ioana, meanwhile, told us in no uncertain terms that the free movement has been beneficial and even necessary to her family:

> What would we do in Romania without having the borders open? How would we live? I had absolutely no opportunity to work there. Here you can make 10–12

euros, you have to work a few days to save them, but still you can send them home. [...] And it's better, the children live better back home, they eat better food and get to have new cloths from time to time. We don't need to become rich. But the children live better and don't lack so many things at the school. So that eventually they can have a better life than us.

## Conclusion

In this article, we have examined the politics and dynamics of the Eastern European Roma migration in Helsinki as a case study of processes of re-bordering and everyday gatekeeping in Europe. We have sought to bring together perspectives on the lives of the Roma migrants, and the shifting policies and institutional engagements.

Since 2007, the migration of small groups of Eastern European Roma has sparked reactions by the public as well as by various level Finnish authorities. The presence of legitimate yet unwanted EU citizens outside labour market has produced a policy dilemma, in which state actors have been unable to form consistent policies in the face of dire social problems. What has in practice emerged is a "policy of no policy", in which the onus of acting has been left to local level. In the city of Helsinki, the municipal authorities have sought to deter the migrants through innovating indirect bordering techniques. Central in this has been the mobilizing of local executive authorities as gatekeepers, on areas such as evictions of campsites, restricting access to emergency accommodation and the use of child protection as a tool or restricting immigration. In the absence of consistent policies, NGOs and civil society actors have become activated, and also mobilized by the City of Helsinki, which has funded the drop-in centre Hirundo in order to provide a minimum support for Roma migrants, while stopping short from inclusive policies.

On the local level, morally and institutionally ambiguous landscapes have emerged in which the fear of giving "incentives" for further migration is juxtaposed with a fear of people "freezing to death" on the streets of Helsinki. Street-level authorities from local police to health care providers and social workers face moral and legal grey zones and potential institutional conflicts in their dealings with the migrants.

Meanwhile, from the migrants' perspective, the ambiguous intersecting policies of the City of Helsinki, Finland and EU have produced a shifting borderscape, with a set of constraints, risks and possibilities which they have adapted to. Everyday bordering and the lack work and housing make Finland into an economically, legally and physically insecure environment. Yet, many of the migrants who we interviewed have been able to utilize adaptive family economies, multiple sources of income and informal networks in order to not only cope with everyday bordering, but also to achieve tangible improvements in their lives.

The politics of Roma migration in Finland point to a combination of racialized othering and institutional contradictions connected to the evolving European citizenship. Our case study points to the modern borderscapes as "moral constructs rich with panic, danger, and patriotism" (Rajaram and Grundy-Warr 2007), and to a tension between purportedly free European mobility and the increasingly selective and securitized politics of immigration.

## Notes

1. In addition, Enache has conducted fieldwork at the Bacau region, Romania, and in Helsinki in 2014 under the research project *Families on the Move across Borders: Children's Perspectives on Migration in Europe*, together with Dr, Airi Markkanen. Moreover, she has been employed as an outreach worker and service coordinator with an organization that provides support for the EU migrants. Both researchers have also volunteered for initiatives organized with the migrants. We are acutely aware of the power asymmetries and ethical challenges our multiple roles give rise to. No confidential discussions, counseling sessions or staff-related information were used in the ethnography. We have strove to use what Yuval-Davis (1997) conceptualises as transversal approach, recognizing power asymmetries and situated positionalities but seeking also to establish common values and aims.
2. Numerous groups of Roma migrants arrived already 1990–2006, including asylum-seekers from ex-Yugoslavia, Slovakia, Czech Republic, Poland, Lithuania, Bulgaria and Romania. Finland responded to this perceived "flood" by re-imposing visa requirements on Slovakian citizens and creating an accelerated procedure for handling applications from "safe" countries, including EU accession countries (cf. Nordberg 2004; Salmenhaara 2010).
3. Starting in 2014, the City of Helsinki provided urgent medical care for undocumented people in the same way as for anyone residing in Helsinki, extending coverage to EU citizens without health insurance.
4. In a rare case of direct bordering, Helsinki's social board paid in 2011 a return-home money to migrants left without shelter by evictions. The experiment was widely considered a failure as many of the migrants immediately returned.
5. When minors have arrive, there have been cases in which they were barred from entering primary school education if their parents did not have permanent address and residence permit (Korniloff and Laine 2014, 11).
6. They do not conform to the notion of precarious workers either, in the sense of forming a workforce whose need to maintain legal status would subjugate them to exploitative employers (Anderson 2010).
7. Individual migrants have worked with cleaning apartments, mending cars and clearing courtyards of snow. The *Hirundo* centre employs Roma workers with temporary contracts, and has sought to connect the migrants with employers.

## Acknowledgements

We are indebted to our interviewees for their trust and patience. We would like to thank Georgie Wemyss, Kathryn Cassidy, Nira Yuval-Davis, Lena Näre, Jukka Könönen, Jan Grill and the anonymous reviewers for their helpful comments and insights, and Maria Dorofte, Elisabeth Wide, Laura Assmuth, Airi Markkanen, Kimmo Grangvist and Aino Saarinen for their help in various stages of the work.

## Disclosure statement

No potential conflict of interest was reported by the authors.

## Funding

This work was supported by the European Commission's Seventh Framework Programme [290775]; The Academy of Finland [284178, 288552]; and the Koneen Säätiö.

## References

Anderson, B. 2010. "Migration, Immigration Controls and the Fashioning of Precarious Workers." *Work Employment & Society* 24: 300–317. doi:10.1177/0950017010362141.

Benedik, S. 2010. "Harming 'Cultural Feelings': Images and Categorisation of Temporary Romani Migrants to Graz/Austria." In *Multi-disciplinary Approaches to Romany Studies*, edited by Michael Stewart, and Márton Rövid, 71–90. Budapest: Central European University Press.

Bigo, D., S. Carrera, and E. Guild. 2013. *Foreigners, Refugees or Minorities? Rethinking People in the Context of Border Controls and Visas*. Wey Court East: Ashgate.

Brochmann, G., and A. Hagelund. 2011. "Migrants in the Scandinavian Welfare State. The Emergence of a Social Policy Problem." *Nordic Journal of Migration Research*, 1 (1): 13–24. doi:10.2478/v10202-011-0003-3.

Bunescu, I. 2014. *Roma in Europe, The Politics of Collective Identity Formation*. Wey Court East: Ashgate.

City of Helsinki. 2011. *Linjauksia kerjäläisongelman käsittelemiseksi Helsingissä*. Helsinki: City of Helsinki.

De Genova, N. 2002. "Migrant 'Illegality' and Deportability in Everyday Life." *Annual Review of Anthropology* 31 (4): 419–447. doi:10.1146/annurev.anthro.31.040402. 085432.

Djuve, A. Britt, J. H. Friberg, G. Tyldum, and H. Zhang. 2015. *When Poverty Meets Affluence. Migrants from Romania on the Streets of the Scandinavian Capitals*. Oslo: Fafo.

Enache, A. 2012. "Köyhyyden Kiertokulku –Romanian romanien viimeaikainen muutto Helsinkiin elonjäämisstrategiana." In *Huomio! Romaneja tiellä*, edited by A. Markkanen, H. Puurunen, and A. Saarinen, 42–71. Helsinki: Like.

Enache, A. 2013. "Talouskriisi ajoi romanialaiset siiirtolaiset liikkeelle." *Hyvinvointikatsaus* 1: 30–36.

Engebrigtsen, A. 2014. "Roma 'Activism', the Media and the Space Between the Devil and the Deep Blue Sea." *Acta Ethnographica Hungarica* 59 (1): 223–234. doi:10. 1556/AEthn.59.2014.1.11.

Favell, A. 2014. "The Fourth Freedom: Theories of Migration and Mobilities in 'Neo-Liberal' Europe." *European Journal of Social Theory* 17, 275–289. doi:10.1177/ 1368431014530926.

Fekete, L. 2014. "Europe Against the Roma." *Race & Class* 55 (3): 60–70.

Fontaine, L., and J. Schlumbohm. 2000. "Household Strategies for Survival: An Introduction." In *Household Strategies for Survival 1600–2000: Fission, Faction and*

*Cooperation*, edited by L. Fontaine and J. Schlumbohm, 1–17. International Review of Social History 45 (2000), Supplement 8. Cambridge: Press Syndicate of the University of Cambridge.

Grill, J. 2011. "From Street Busking in Switzerland to Meat Factories in the UK: A Comparative Study of Two Roma Migration Networks from Slovakia." In *Emerging Inequalities in Europe: Poverty and Transnational Migration*, edited by D. Kaneff, and F. Pine, 79–102. London: Anthem Press.

Grill, J. 2012. "Going Up to England: Exploring Mobilities among Roma from Eastern Slovakia." *Journal of Ethnic and Migration Studies*, 38 (8): 1269–1287. doi:10.1080/1369183X.2012.689187.

Helsinki Deaconess Institute. 2010. *ROM PO DROM -projektin loppuraportti [Roma on the Road-Project Final Report]*. Helsinki: Helsinki Deaconess Institute.

Iacovetta, F. 2006. *Gatekeepers: Reshaping Immigrant Lives in Cold War Canada*. Toronto: In Between the Lines.

Jokela, M. 2016. "Marginaalit kaupunkitilassa. Tapaustutkimus sosiaalikeskus Satamasta." *Sosiologia*. In print (accepted for publishing 13 Apr 2016).

Korniloff, M., and M. Laine. 2014. *Paperittoman lapsen oikeus perusopetukseen* [Paperless children's right to primary education]. Helsinki: Paperittomat –hanke, Pakolaisneuvonta ry.

Leinonen, T., and M. Vesalainen. 2008. *Päivästä päivään, maasta maahan -tavoitteena toimeentulo*. Helsinki: Helsinki Deaconess Institute.

Lindström, T. 2015. *They Don't Fit In. Homeless EU Migrants, New Social Risks and the Mixed Economy of Welfare in Sweden*. Lund: Lund University.

Lucassen, L. 1997. "'Harmful Tramps': Police Professionalization and Gypsies in Germany, 1700–1945." In *Gypsies and Other Itinerant Groups. A Socio-Historical Approach*, edited by L. Lucassen, W. Willems, and A. Cottaar, 74–93. Macmillan: Basingstoke.

Manzoni, C. 2016. "Should I Stay or Should I Go? Why Roma Migrants Leave or Remain in Nomad Camps." *Ethnic and Racial Studies*. 1–18. doi:10.1080/01419870.2016.1201579.

Markkanen, A. 2012. "Romanian romanien elämisen ehdot Suomessa ja Romaniassa – onko romaneille tilaa EU-Euroopassa?" In *Huomio! Romaneja tiellä*, edited by A. Markkanen, H. Puurunen, and A. Saarinen, 72–104. Helsinki: Like.

Mezzadra, S., and B. Neilson. 2013. *Border as Method, or, the Multiplication of Labor*. Durham: Duke University Press Books.

Nacu, A. 2011. "The Politics of Roma Migration: Framing Identity Struggles among Romanian and Bulgarian Roma in the Paris Region." *Journal of Ethnic and Migration Studies*, 37 (1): 135–150. doi:10.1080/1369183X.2010.515134.

Näre, L. 2011. "The Informal Economy of Paid Domestic Work: Ukrainian and Polish Migrants in Naples." In *Foggy Social Structures. Irregular Migration*, edited by M. Bommes and G. Sciortino, European Labour Markets and the Welfare State, 67–87. Amsterdam: Amsterdam University Press.

Nordberg, C. 2004. "Legitimising Immigration Control: Romani Asylum-Seekers in the Finnish Debate." *Journal of Ethnic and Migration Studies*, 30 (4): 717–735. doi:10.1080/1369183040001699531.

Picker, G. 2013. "That Neighbourhood Is an Ethnic Bomb!' The Emergence of an Urban Governance Apparatus in Western Europe." *European Urban and Regional Studies* 0 (0): 1–13. doi:10.1177/0969776413502659.

Portes, A., M. Castells, and L. Benton, eds. 1989. *The Informal Economy: Studies in Advanced and Less Developed Countries*. Baltimore, MD: John Hopkins University Press.

Puurunen, H., A. Enache, and A. Markkanen. 2016. "Päiväkeskus Hirundo: apua ja tukea itäisen Euroopan romaneille Helsingissä." In *Kansainvälinen sosiaalityö: käsitteitä ja käytäntöjä meiltä ja muualta*, edited by M. Jäppinen, A. Metteri, S. Ranta-Tyrkkö, and P. Rauhala, 227–245. Tallinna: United Press Global.

Rajaram, P. K., and C. Grundy-Warr. 2007. *Borderscapes: Hidden Geographies and Politics at Territory's Edge*. Minneapolis: University of Minnesota Press.

Roman, R. 2014. "Transnational Migration and the Issue of 'Ethnic' Solidarity. Finnish Roma Elite and Eastern European Roma Migrants in Finland." *Ethnicities*, 14 (6): 793–810. doi:10.1177/1468796814542179.

Salmenhaara, P. 2010. "A Case Study of Finnish Deportations: The Shymansky Case 2002." *Finnish Journal of Ethnicity and Migration*, 5 (1): 50–59.

Sigona, N. 2011. "The Governance of Romani People in Italy: Discourse, Policy and Practice." *Journal of Modern Italian Studies*, 16 (5): 590–616.

Sigona, N., and N. Trehan. 2009. *Romany Politics in Contemporary Europe: Poverty, Ethnic Mobilization and the Neoliberal Order*. London: Palgrave Macmillan.

Tervonen, M. 2012. "Syrjäytetyt: lyhyt katsaus romanien yhteiskunnallisen uloslyönnin pitkään historiaan." In *Huomio! Romaneja tiellä*, edited by A. Markkanen, H. Puurunen, and A. Saarinen, 138–148. Helsinki: Like.

Tervonen, M. 2016. "The Nordic Passport Union and Its Discontents: Unintended Consequences of Free Movement." In *Nordic Cooperation: A European Region in Transition*, edited by Johan Strang, 131–146. London: Routledge.

Trehan, N. 2009. "The Romani Subaltern within Neoliberal European Civil Society: NGOization of Human Rights and Silent Voices." In *Romany Politics in Contemporary Europe: Poverty, Ethnic Mobilization and the Neoliberal Order*, edited by N. Sigona and N. Trehan, 51–71. London: Palgrave Macmillan.

Van Baar, H. 2014. "The Centripetal Dimension of the EU's External Border Regime." *Etnofoor: Anthropological Journal* 26 (2): 87–93.

Vesterberg, V. 2016. "Exploring Misery Discourses: Problematized Roma in Labour Market Projects." *European Journal for Research on the Education and Learning of Adults* 7 (1): 25–40.

Vitale, T. 2008. "Contestualizzare l'azione pubblica: ricerca del consenso e varietà di strumenti nelle politiche locali per i rom e i sinti." In *I rom e l'azione* [Roma and action], edited by G. Bezzecchi, M. Pagani, and T. Vitale, 7–42. Milano: Teti editore.

Vitale, T., and O. Legros. 2011. ""Les migrants roms dans les villes françaises et ita-liennes: mobilités, régulations et marginalités" [The migrant Roma in French and Italian cities: mobilities, regulation and marginality]." *Géocarrefour* 86 (1): 3–14.

Vlase, I., and M. Voicu. 2013. "Romanian Roma Migration: The Interplay Between Structures and Agency." *Ethnic and Racial Studies*, 37 (13): 2418–2437. doi:10.1080/01419870.2013.809133.

Willems, W. 1998. "Ethnicity as a Death-trap: The History of Gypsy Studies." In *Gypsies and Other Itinerant Groups, A Socio-Historical Approach*, edited by L. Lucassen, W. Willems, and A. Cottaar, 17–34. Macmillan: Basingstoke.

Yuval-Davis, N. 1997. *Gender and Nation*. London: Sage.

Yuval-Davis, N. 2013. "A Situated Intersectional Everyday Approach to the Study of Bordering." EUborderscapes Working Paper 2. (www.euborderscapes.eu/fileadmin/user_upload/Working_Papers/EUBORDERSCAPES_Working_Paper_2_Yuval-Davis.pdf).

# "People think that Romanians and Roma are the same": everyday bordering and the lifting of transitional controls

Georgie Wemyss and Kathryn Cassidy

**ABSTRACT**

On 1 January 2014 the transitional controls on free movement adopted by the UK when Bulgaria and Romania joined the EU in 2007, ended. This paper demonstrates how the discourses of politicians relating to their removal, amplified via news media contributed to the extension of state bordering practices further into everyday life. Based on ethnographic research into everyday bordering during 2013–15 the paper uses an intersectional framework to explore how this homogenizing, bordering discourse was experienced and contested from differently situated perspectives of Roma and non-Roma social actors from established communities.

## Introduction

On 1 January 2014 the local *KentOnline* headline stated that the County Council leader was "set for thousands of migrants from Bulgaria and Romania as working restrictions lifted". The opening paragraph read:

> More pressure will be put on Kent's education, health and crime workers as thousands of Bulgarians and Romanians are expected to come into the county over the next few years.

> That's the message from the leader of Kent County Council [ … ], as the county sees working restrictions for those countries lifted from today.

> Despite the Government implementing tough new benefit restrictions on migrants who wish to live and work in Britain, [ … ] believes Kent is still an attractive option for young Bulgarian and Romanian workers who wish to earn higher wages.[1]

Below was a picture captioned "Three Roma children in Romania". Later on in the same article a local woman stated:

> I am concerned about the restrictions being lifted, many of them are taking council homes from people like myself. "We can't get on the council list to get a house, because they are being offered to foreigners first. [2]

This report signalled the end of "transitional controls" for Romania and Bulgaria (known as the "A2" countries) that had joined the European Union seven years earlier. Transitional controls are one of a range of everyday state bordering technologies used to restrict the access that citizens of European Union countries have to the UK labour market and welfare benefits. Whilst the EU legislation that established these controls does not discriminate between the ethnicities and genders of citizens of specified countries, this paper demonstrates how the discourses of politicians, amplified via news media contributes to the extension of state bordering practices further into the everyday lives of Roma and non-Roma UK residents.

Following an introduction to the concept of "everyday bordering", the paper traces the context to the removal of the transitional controls on A2 migrants to the UK. After a methodological discussion, the paper then examines political and media discourses in the period prior to January 2014. The subsequent section draws on ethnographic interviews to explore how a number of social actors across London and the South East including Slovak Roma, non-Roma Romanian and Slovak and local white women and men from established communities including public sector professionals – differentially experienced and contested these discourses.[3]

## Everyday bordering

Border studies over the last two decades has been characterized by two key developmental avenues: theoretical developments which have increasingly come to frame them as complex processes rather than static lines at the edge of nation-states (Brambilla 2015); and shifting political and policy agendas in the Minority World, which have moved border controls away from geographical borders and into the everyday life of communities within these states (Balibar 2002). Consequently, scholars have been responding to a growing need to understand both their proliferating forms and practices (Green 2013) and the ways in which they have become embedded in everyday life (Johnson et al. 2011; Johnson and Jones 2014). For the UK, this has led to an increase in legislation since the mid-1990s, which has multiplied state-sponsored bordering practices within society. In this everyday context, ordinary people have become involved in "borderwork" (Rumford 2008) as agents of the state or as Vaughan-Williams (2008) argues in the role of the "citizen-detective". In the UK, such roles are enforced by punitive regimes including fines levied against employers, landlords, health and educational institutions. Transitional controls imposed on A2 nationals by the UK in 2007 formed part of this policy agenda of what we term "everyday bordering" (Yuval-Davis et al. forthcoming). In exploring state bordering in its everyday context we follow de Certeau's (1984) argument that in cultural productions the everyday functions as the foundational context for practices that clearly move beyond the everyday. It is within this construction of everyday life that we explore selected practices and discourses surrounding the lifting of transitional controls as racialized forms of everyday bordering, which have had a particular impact on Roma in the UK.

## Transitional controls

When Romania and Bulgaria joined the European Union in January 2007 the British government placed controls on labour market engagement for Romanian and Bulgarian (A2) nationals coming to the UK. Unlike those who had come to the UK exercising treaty rights following the 2004 (A8) enlargement, A2 nationals were restricted in accessing both the labour market and state welfare benefits. The use of transitional controls had arisen as a response to the migration of high numbers of A8 nationals after the 2004 enlargement and an approach towards border securitization, which had been increasing in the UK since the 1990s involving the movement of policing the UK's border away from border crossing points and into the heart of communities across Britain. A2 nationals had to gain worker authorization for employment and after twelve months of paid employment were discharged from the scheme and gained the "right to reside", which enabled them to claim state benefits. A2 nationals also had to pass the Habitual Residence Test, (HBT) which in addition to "right to reside" sought to establish intention to remain in the UK for the foreseeable future. Without the "right to reside" A2 and A8 nationals had no recourse to public funds. To continue this approach following the removal of the controls, the UK government again enacted the "right to reside" mechanism in the 2014 Immigration Act. This legislation gave EU nationals looking for work in the UK access to Universal Credit (which is gradually replacing a range of welfare benefits) for three months. If they fail to find work in this period they do not gain the "right to reside" and are unable to access state support. Those who find work have the "right to reside" after this period and are able to claim benefits, such as Child Benefit.[4] Poole and Adamson (2008, 33) describe this approach as consistent with those taken by previous British governments in that it attempted to "maximise the benefits of labour migration without incurring its costs".

In addition to the differentiated categories of EU nationals created by the transitional controls, the impact of these controls is also filtered through the situated gazes of those who administer them and of differently situated migrants (Yuval-Davis 2013). This paper examines the complexity of these processes as well as their sometimes abstract sometimes very concrete nature, that could lead to the label of "the border multiple", composed of multifarious, contested and contradictory narratives at different levels of practice. They include individuals and the practices of their everyday lives as well as discursive-material actors which can collude, contest and interfere with each other across or on the same side of the border (Johnson and Jones 2014, 5–7). In this paper we are arguing that whilst transitional controls continue to be visible technologies of the state bordering regime aimed at restricting access to the UK labour market of citizens of specified EU member states, the negative political and media discourses that contributed to their implementation when Romania and Bulgaria joined the EU in 2007 and surrounded their ending on the first of January 2014 worked as a bordering process to exclude Roma already settled in Britain and potential Roma migrants regardless of citizenship. These hegemonic discourses were experienced in the day to day lives of Slovak Roma and non-Roma settled in Dover as well as Romanian migrant workers settled in London.

## Methodology

The data in this article were gathered around the specific "ethnographic moment" of the ending of transitional controls on New Year's Day 2014 that occurred during the wider EUBorderscapes research project that covered the period 2013–15. The wider project was focused on a number of different sites, including the Schengen/non-Schengen territorial border of Dover/Calais and two boroughs in the London metropolis. The study began in the run up to local elections in Dover in May 2013, seven months before the ending of transitional controls and continued through the EU and London local elections five months after their ending. It finished soon after the UK general election one year later. The punctuation of the two years by local, national and supranational elections gave us the opportunity to observe how discourses about Roma migration to the UK in national media were experienced differently at varied times by local Roma and non-Roma residents and professionals who interacted with local Roma. In order to understand their complex experiences, we employed a situated, intersectional analysis that accounts for different views or "situated gazes", by exploring how the varying positionality of social agents is connected to their relationships with different social, economic and political projects. To capture these complex negotiations, we use what McCall (2005) calls inter- and intra-categorical approaches. The inter-categorical approach focuses on the way the intersection of different social categories, such as race, gender and class affect particular social behaviour or distribution of resources. However, our study also pays attention to intra-categorical processes, which are concerned with the shaping of the meanings and boundaries of the categories themselves.

As we collected ethnographic data relating to UK state borders, including participant observation, focus groups and interviews of differently positioned Roma and non-Roma UK residents and analysed local and national media discourses, the everyday bordering processes of not only the instruments of the transitional controls but also, significantly, the political and media discourses surrounding the ending of those controls emerged as key issues amongst many participants. We were able to explore how different groups entered into dialogue with media and public discourses that emerged about the ending of the transitional controls. The analysis combines a Foucauldian theorization of the dominant discourse as a "regime of truth" (1980, 131) employed by Clark and Campbell in their media analysis of UK press discourses about Czech and Slovak "asylum seekers" at a particular moment in 1997 (2000) with Gramsci's dynamic notion of "common sense" (1971) achieved through struggles between forms of knowledge associated with competing groups.

In this paper we focus on the situated intersectional gazes of a range of individuals affected by political and media discourses that peaked around the ending of transitional controls for A2 citizens on New Year's Day 2014. We were able to explore how, at the moment of the ending of the transitional controls, political and media discourses extended their reach, working as everyday, filtering bordering processes before and after their withdrawal.

## Everyday bordering: political and media discourses surrounding the end of the transitional controls

The everyday bordering processes of transitional controls, whilst rooted in UK and EU equality legislation have been targeted at, and experienced differently, by diverse citizens of A8 and A2 countries as well as by people from the Global South who have settled across Europe and moved to the UK. In this section we draw on critical discourse analysis (Fairclough 1995) to track and analyse some of the key political and media discourses in the run up to and after January 2014. In focusing on the contexts of these discourses we show how they work to extend the border further into everyday life. In examining the texts and how they are contested, we contribute to debates that frame hostility against Roma as an expression of historical anxieties about immigration or of contemporary concerns about the principle to free movement in the EU and that question the taken for granted homogeneity of Roma populations (Guy 2003; Guy, Uherek, and Weinrova 2004; Sigona and Trehan 2009; Bunescu 2014).

In this paper, temporality is central to the understanding of bordering discourses in two significant aspects. First, in terms of dominant political and media discourses, the time frame of electoral cycles leads to peaks in the immigration "scare stories" which impact on the everyday lives and situated gazes of those who are associated with those negative representations. Several studies have shown that repetitive media discourses about the "crisis" of asylum and refugees, including Roma, have influenced government to introduce policies that aim to limit the number of asylum seekers in the UK (Clark and Campbell 2000, 42; Guy 2004; Philo, Briant, and Donald 2013, 7). A range of participants in public sector meetings, interviews and focus groups commented on media discourses about the lifting of transitional controls building up during 2013 to peak as their ending approached and as the political campaigns around the 2014 European elections developed. Secondly, each phase of migration informs the situated gaze of those who have experienced earlier phases of migration and associated discourses. Border narratives in the media, created from complex and chaotic events shape viewer/reader's perception of the border as well as those who cross and enforce it, they tend to invisibilise the historical, socio-economic and political contexts of migrants' lives (Jones 2014). Therefore, in understanding the Roma and non-Roma situated gaze in relation to discourses and technologies of everyday bordering, we include in the analysis the historical context of past life experiences as well as negative media discourses about the Roma in local, UK national and other European media as discussed by Yuval-Davis et al. in this special issue.

## National media and the end of transitional controls

In the run up to the ending of transitional controls, a BBC report referred to a "storm of British media coverage and political debate over an expected surge in immigration from Bulgaria and Romania" (BBC News website, December 18, 2013). The "storm" included headlines from the tabloid press that accompanied photographs of anonymous "immigrants" at passport controls. Whilst some, such as those below, did not include references to "Roma", many included pictures which were either captioned as being of Roma people or used photographs of people who fitted a visible stereotype of "Roma".[5]

> A TIDAL wave of Romanian and Bulgarian immigrants is threatening to swamp Britain — and flood our overstretched jobs market.
>
> An EU law means that from 2014, more than 29 million people from the two countries will be entitled to apply for any UK job. (*The Sun*, November 2013)
>
> 385,000 Romanians and Bulgarians will flock to UK
>
> AT LEAST 385,000 migrants from Romania and Bulgaria will head to Britain to find work over the next five years, a new report claimed yesterday. (*The Daily Express*, December 2013)[6]

Echoing an earlier, process whereby the words "refugees" and asylum seeker' became "generic terms for what is perceived as bad behaviour by new groups of people" (Philo, Briant, and Donald 2013, 133) in 2013–14 the discursive slippage between the categories of "Bulgarian", "Romanian" and "Roma", via the juxtaposition of headlines and photographs with words and images that suggest Roma otherness, poverty and criminality have contributed towards them becoming generic negative terms for an undesirable group around which the scare stories are spun.[7] In the following section we examine how this discourse about the ending of transitional controls was reproduced in local contexts and the specific similarities and contrasts in the ways it was experienced by differently situated Roma and non-Roma residents.

## Conflation and contest: dominant discourse surrounding the ending of transitional controls and the situated intersectional gaze

We begin with examples drawn from Kent where the contemporary perspectives of residents need to be understood in the context of earlier Roma migrations. As Yuval-Davis et al. mention in this special issue, Roma from the Czech Republic and Slovakia first arrived as asylum seekers in Dover following the break-up of Czechoslovakia in 1993. Some lost their asylum claims and were deported whilst others stayed and were later joined by family members. After the 2004 EU enlargement, some of those previously deported returned and others came and settled in Dover, many working in a local factory and as cleaners. Local Roma and non-Roma told us that they chose Dover because their families already felt settled there and it was accessible for annual trips home. During that period Dover became increasingly diverse as A8 migrants found work and men from, for example, Iraqi Kurdistan and Afghanistan claimed asylum and settled. The legislative ending of the bordering mechanism of transitional controls did not directly affect the Roma community living in Dover and Folkestone since they were citizens of A8 countries. However, their lives were impacted by the political and media discourses, such as the examples above that used their presence in Dover to imply that greater numbers of Roma from Bulgaria and Romania would migrate to the area after 1 January 2014. In the context of Kent, the conflation of diverse populations of different nationalities into a single category of "Roma" associated with specific social "problems" was reproduced in a local council report that, building on earlier and existing discourses (Clark and Campbell 2000; Guy 2003, 2004), made generalizing statements about Roma communities. It was picked up by local and national media, whose coverage was contested by diverse state and NGO-employees as well as by local Slovak Roma whose everyday lives were directly impacted. In this section we explore how this discourse was reproduced, experienced and contested by these differently situated actors.

## Local government report: the contested situated gaze of the political leadership

In April 2013 Conservative and UK Independence Party (UKIP) councillors of Kent County Council (KCC) commissioned a report into potential additional demand on local services arising from the ending of transitional employment restrictions on A2 countries (Kent County Council 2013). The report drew on experience of post 2004 A8 migration in Kent to plan future impacts. Whilst the report was focused on Romanian and Bulgarian migration generally, specific references to Roma migration made assumptions about Roma cultural homogeneity[8] and included estimates of the total Roma populations of Europe, the two A2 countries and the UK. [9] Another referred to discrimination experienced by Roma, patterns of chain migration and the extra resources their migration may require from public bodies.[10] Further paragraphs focused on Roma involvement in child trafficking[11] and the role of the media in reducing misinformation about Roma, referring enquiries to the KCC's own Gypsy and Traveller Unit.

Labour and Liberal Democrat councillors opposed the report as "pointless" and "electioneering", one argued that reliable information was not available locally or nationally and another that the announcement of its commissioning was linked to the local elections two weeks later (BBC Kent April, 2013).[12] The councillors' concerns about the reliability of data on Roma was shared by the authors of a report commissioned by Home Office funded South East Partnership for Migration (SEPM) from November 2013. This report into the profile and distribution of A2 migrants in the South East explicitly avoided generalizations in not mentioning Roma migration beyond the introduction to its remit:

> A key concern for many local authorities in the South East particularly relates to the inflow of Roma community members. Given that the key data sources that this report draws on do not include information to separate out such migrants, no attempt has been made to specifically address Roma migration. As well as responding to economic and network drivers of migration, Roma communities also adjust to discrimination and racism across Europe. (Nygaard, Pasierbek, and Francis-Brophy 2013, 3)

The report demonstrated that whilst local authorities wanted to address specifically Roma migration the researchers were not willing to do so due to lack of data.[13]

## Media amplification: extending the gaze of the political leadership

The KCC report was cited on 1 January 2014 in the *KentOnline* article above. In that article, as well as the use of images of Roma children in Romania, references to the report were interspersed with quotes from the commissioner of the report, the leader of KCC that slipped into direct references to Roma as a "problem". For example:

> Politicians and councillors in Kent have expressed concern that increased migration will only stretch the demand on local government services and could create "township ghettos" in some towns like Maidstone. [Council leader] added: "I think more people looking to work here will only put added pressures on education, health and sadly crime. "A significant amount of criminality is being carried out in parts of Kent by people from Eastern Europe. "Everyone's seen the Roma issues in Boston and in Sheffield, in those places it's putting significant additional burdens on those local authorities and we have a significant problem in East Kent.[14]

The Conservative leader of the council used local media at the moment of the ending of transitional controls to link local Roma with criminality and pressures on welfare, making direct references to negative discourses about Roma elsewhere in Britain. In this case the gaze of the political leader and the local media had much in common. In another example, the SEPM report, which explicitly did not focus on Roma migration, was publicised by the Mail on Sunday using stereotypical "Roma images" familiar since media coverage from the 1990s (Guy 2003, 70). The heading "Exposed: What they DIDN'T tell you about new wave of migrants heading for booming Britain' (Mail on Sunday, December 28 2014), combined references to the report which did not include evidence about Roma with "Roma" images to sharpen the negative focus onto supposedly visibly identifiable Roma people.[15]

### Situated gaze of local borderworkers

The dominant discourses that generalized Roma lives into a homogeneous category which was then conflated with other Eastern European categories was challenged by state and NGO-employees who engaged with local Roma in their everyday work. The A2 migration issue and the KCC report were on the agenda of a meeting attended by local authority and NGO stakeholders in December 2013. The meeting was asked "how are you feeling about the A2 migration issue?" A local government employee said that "the media are trying to whip up a storm that may not happen. They are looking for a teacup". He argued that "Roma are very heterogeneous" and others agreed. Whilst they challenged media assumptions of Roma homogeneity and criminality, some generalizations made in this meeting and in interviews of health and policing professionals shared other strands of the report's discourse. For example, in focusing on discrimination experienced by Roma that acts as a "push factor" and their "lack of compliance" being due to their previous experiences and vulnerability to criminals when they can't find work.

We interviewed local professionals who contrasted their awareness of the complexities of Roma and other minority communities, learned through their everyday work, with the ignorance of the media and of local white people. A long standing Community Liaison Police Officer remarked on a local anti-migrant discourse that groups diverse minorities into the single category of "Slovak":

> There is this general generic term called "Slovak" which relates basically to anyone who is Eastern European. But whether they would differentiate between an asylum seeker, any other sort of migrant, an EU Roma, pretty well not.

> The other day we had a crime report of a guy who verbally abused a Roma. And he said "You bloody Slovaks, why don't you go back to Pakistan?!" and that just sums it up really.

Whilst the police officer pointed out the term "Slovak" was used to abuse diverse minority groups, interviews with local people discussed below demonstrated that it was also used to specifically reference the local Roma population.

### Contrasting gazes of Roma and non-Roma young people

When the media "storm" was at its height in December 2013 we visited a youth club in Folkestone, which worked to integrate local Roma and non-Roma young people. Although youths from both groups used the building on the same evenings, Roma and non-Roma young people rarely mixed. We therefore carried out separate group interviews. Discussing the local area, the white teenage men referred to local Roma, including those who used the same youth club, by their assumed nationalities and in using the labels "Slovak" and "Czech" drew on the familiar discourses of Roma criminality and welfare abuse:

> JS: We get a lot of Slovakians and Czechs. They like to cause trouble.

> NK: Mainly around the Harbour areas of Folkestone that's mainly where they are, that causes quite a lot of crime here.

> JS: If you walk up and down [ … ] Street once or twice a day you see a drug deal. Or prostitution, yeah. Quite a few of them just scrounge off the government.

Not surprisingly the perspectives of the Roma young people in the youth club challenged such discourses. GN, a teenage Slovak Roma female college student came to join her parents working as cleaners in 2005. Her spoken English was indistinguishable from the non-Roma young people in the youth club. In earlier parts of the discussion she had spoken about how, in contrast to her experiences in Slovakia, she did not have racist teachers in Kent. However, her experiences of racism differed depending on whom she was with:

> When I started being more with English people at college and stuff, I'd go out with them, no-one looks at me differently when I am with them, but when **we**

are in a group like now, um, that's when it gets hard, when **we** are in a group [her emphasis].

GN was referring to racist comments that she was subjected to when with other local young Roma people. As part of a diverse group of students (whom she referred to as "English") she was able to avoid the negative meanings associated with the label of "Roma" or Slovak'.[16] However this changed whenever her "Roma" identity became visible when with family and Roma friends. Referring to local people's reactions to media reports about the ending of transitional controls she said:

> ... they don't care where you are from, they don't care whether you are Romanian, they are just racist to anyone and when they see something on the news that is why it affects **us** as well. It doesn't matter if it is about Romanian people because they think it is **us** as well and they say to **us** "you are getting our money" so it does affect **us** [her emphasis].

From GN's perspective, the media discourses about A2 migration that conflated "Romanian" with "Roma" into a single negative and historically visible category directly affected her community's experiences of racism.

### Contrasting gaze: Slovak Roma and Slovak non-Roma women

During a focus group discussion, Slovak Roma women in Dover reflected on the impact of media reports about Bulgarians and Romanians in the period running up to the end of transitional controls.[17] Like the young Roma woman above, they noted an impact on them, particularly in relation to presumed criminality:

> T and others: We feel that store detectives are suspecting us and following us around the shops and it is very unpleasant, and the second thing is the people think that Romanians and Roma are the same people because we look similar, but it is far from the case [ ... ].
>
> Interviewer: Did this happen before as well?
>
> T and others: It never happened to me before.

One woman suggested that the negative media was impacting on the ability of Roma to gain access to paid work through a particular employment agency:

> They also have more strict criteria about who and when to register to the agency for employment. I am not going to name the agency, in my personal experience, but I know that they are now more fussy about the people they register there.

The perspectives of other Slovaks in professional employment reveal different experiences to the Roma women above. KS is a non-Roma, Slovak women, who has been living and working with local Roma people in Dover for a number of years. She suggested that she has shared some of their racist experiences:

> I took a taxi once, I still have quite a strong accent I think, and the taxi driver asked me where I was from, and I said Slovakia and the taxi driver asked me to leave the taxi.

In this case she had stated her background and been questioned by the driver based on her accent. This differs from the experiences of the Roma women, who found themselves harassed on shopping trips because of assumptions around criminality based on their appearance. In contrast to Roma experiences of the period leading up to the removal of the transitional controls KS stated "I haven't noticed to tell the truth, I haven't noticed at all", suggesting that KS' whiteness shaped her gaze towards the removal of the controls as being unproblematic. AC, a Czech woman living in Dover, was critical of the focus on Roma and criminality in the local media:

> In the local newspaper there were some articles in the past about Slovak Roma but no one was very positive. They were only about problems about rowdiness, rubbish, criminal offences, fraud and so on.

She referred specifically to Slovak Roma in a way that both contested other local white discourses that grouped all outsiders together as "Slovaks" and situated herself outside of that category. This process of Roma othering was shared by non-Roma Romanians in London, who under the glare of the media discourses surrounding the ending of the transitional controls, also developed strong discourses excluding Roma from their own national project of belonging.

### Non-Roma Romanian gaze

The discourses associated with the removal of transitional controls were experienced in complex ways by non-Roma Romanians in London. Media representations of Romanians in the period prior to the removal of the transitional controls led to heightened anti-Roma discourses amongst non-Roma Romanians (see also Pusca 2010). These discourses reflected a Romanian national project of belonging, which historically excludes the Roma and highlights the racism many encounter in Romania. Away from the glare of the media there was often a high level of ambiguity surrounding the definitions of Roma/non-Roma. The wider political and media discourses surrounding transitional controls had initiated the emergence of new forms of everyday counter-discourse, which due to the particular situated gazes of the non-Roma migrant workers, were grounded in the historical exclusion of Roma in Romanian society. For these workers, Roma came to embody threats to their freedom to move and, consequently, their livelihoods (Pusca 2010; Guillem 2011).

In October 2013, we visited SS, a Romanian woman who had moved to London in 2008. During a visit from her younger brother (AS) they were watching a news item on UK television about the end of transitional controls.

> AS: I don't understand why they always show pictures of "gypsies" (tigani). Do they think all Romanians are gypsies?

> SS: Yes, everyone at work thinks we all live like those pictures they show of gypsies in Romania. They think we have nothing. Seriously, my work colleagues think I live in some kind of shed. I don't tell them I have a house and land there. They think we are all living like gypsies.

SS' comment revealed that the discourses were impacting on her interactions with colleagues evidencing the role of everyday bordering technology in disrupting relations in multicultural communities. Later that month, whilst watching television at AS' apartment, there was a report on the UK news about the Romanian Roma from Botosani who had been removed but returned to Marble Arch. AS became frustrated throughout the broadcast, saying:

> They're gypsies, not Romanians! Why are they calling them Romanians? Every time I see Romanians on television here or a programme that is supposed to be about Romanians, when I watch it there are always gypsies. OK, sometimes there are Romanians as well, but they are mostly gypsies, because these are the people who are stealing and begging for money. This is what they want you to think of Romanians. [ ... ]

AS echoed many of the comments and everyday racism aimed at Roma people in Romania, where they are characterized as lazy, workshy and thieves as justifications for exclusion from the Romanian national project of belonging (Pusca 2010). This is evident in the meanings embedded in the Romanian verb "to gypsy oneself".[18] In contrast our informants did not use that verb to describe another Romanian national, who systematically exploited them through his employment agency.

During the period prior to the removal of the transitional controls there was an intensification of discourses amongst non-Roma stressing the non-belonging of Roma in Romanian society. Yet there was no reflection or recognition of the exclusion and marginalization Roma suffered within Romania.[19] In spite of the very strong discourses of non-belonging present in Romania and which emerged during the period prior to the removal of transitional controls in the UK, when not discussing this issue or responding to media representations of Romanians, there was often significant ambiguity in how Romanians living in London referred to Roma. This illustrates that it was the broader political and media discourses that were shaping counter-narratives. DZ, a young Romanian man, had moved to the Newham from South London in 2013. He and AS discussed finding a new place to live:

DZ: I spoke to the gypsy about moving back into his place. He said he has a free place.

AS: I thought you said he wasn't a gypsy but his wife is?

DZ: Well he doesn't look it but he is a sort of gypsy, you know? He's sly [*smecher*] like a gypsy.

Whilst many Romanians would claim to "know" Roma from their appearance (this was often the means for identifying Roma in the media representations described above), here this is not the case. DZ claimed to know the man is Roma due to his character. However, there was another reason for him considering his former landlord to be Roma and that was his wife. Again, suggesting that Roma and non-Roma are mutually exclusive categories and denying that a Romanian would be married to a Roma woman is part of an understanding, which sets Roma apart from Romanians. Such marriages were considered to be taboo in some Romanian communities. ER was a migrant sex worker, who came to London for six months each year to work. In March 2014, she explained why she was frequently isolated from her peers:

> You know I am a gypsy? Well my husband is a gypsy. Some of the other girls they don't like that but [her friend] is OK.

ER considered herself to be Roma through marriage and the other women treated her as if she were Roma, with many of them refusing to speak to her or work the same area. Whilst many of the Romanian street sex workers looked after one another, ER was excluded from these networks by all but one woman.

Media representations of Romanians in the period prior to the removal of the transitional controls had a clear impact on Romanians living in London. Discourses of non-belonging for Roma embedded in the historic exclusion of Roma in Romania itself (Woodcock 2007) emerged. Nationally, these discourses reflected a supposed threat to Romania's very place within the EU, for Romanians living in London the concerns surrounded the impact these representations had upon their relationships and interactions with British people in everyday life. As such, the emergent anti-Roma narratives were an attempt to counter media representations, which were dominated by the poverty and criminality of Romanians living in the UK. Nonetheless, as we have shown, away from the context of media representation, there was greater ambiguity surrounding discourses of Roma/non-Roma amongst Romanians living in London, which pointed to complexities in defining Roma as separate or distinguishable from Romanians as a group.

## Conclusions

We began this paper with the concept of everyday bordering and describing transitional controls and welfare regulations as filtering state border technologies that work to create divisions and inequalities by restricting access to the labour market for "less desirable" EU migrants. We then showed how these technologies work in conjunction with powerful discourses about their ending, to extend the border more deeply into the everyday lives of EU migrants and most intrusively into the lives of Roma residents. What emerges are specific and closely related processes of everyday bordering, which weave together the past, present and future in the ways in which the actors interviewed responded to and often attempted to challenge. In his analysis of "Border Wars" the documentary-style show about the US Border Patrol, Jones (2014) noted the disjuncture between the official representations of a "clean picture of right and wrong and good and evil at the border" that structured the series and the glimpses of complex lives of diverse individuals and families, pursued by the Border Patrol, as they sought better lives across borders. He concluded that "in 'Border Wars' there are two competing stories of the border; which image remains in the mind is open to question" (2014, 203). The dominant media discourses about the ending of the border technology of transitional controls for A2 migrants also included two connected narratives, which conflated the heterogeneous fuzzy categories of Romanian and Roma into a homogeneous, fixed category of "Roma". One narrative focused on Roma criminality and welfare abuse in the UK and the other on poverty and discrimination in their home countries. Using intersectional analysis to understand the gaze of a range of differently situated people, we have not only shown which stories about A2 migration "remain in the mind" of Roma and non-Roma individuals but also the diverse and complex ways that they experience and contest the repetition of those racialized bordering narratives in their everyday lives.

The paper indicates how the symbolic use of "Roma" in political and media discourses works as a discriminatory bordering process to exclude both non-Romanian Roma and non-Roma Romanian EU citizens from experiencing belonging in their local communities. In the context of the 2014 European Elections and the national media focus on the ending of transitional controls, local politicians in Kent sought to demonstrate to the electorate that they were addressing the "Roma issue" but were unable to do so directly due to the invisibility of valid "Roma" statistical data. Nonetheless, the discourses around the ending of transitional controls became racialized through broad statements about "Roma" populations in the KCC report and in the media coverage of it and other reports, through the use of photographs of "Roma" that resonated with earlier reporting and experiences of local populations. The impact of these racializing discourses was more acute on the everyday lives of local Roma Slovak women than on local white Slovak women. Whilst it attempted to challenge some of the stereotypes, there was discursive continuity between the KCC report and the views about Czech and Slovak Roma expressed by the white young people in Folkestone. For Romanians in

London, the reporting of the ending of the controls had shifted their relationships with their colleagues and led to frustration, anger and anti-Roma discourses, often embedded in those permeating Romanian society. This was in spite of the fact that there was, at times, recognition of the heterogeneity and distinct ambiguity surrounding Roma and non-Roma.

Our examples emphasize the ways in which such wider discourses are not innocuous and have direct but differential impacts upon the way that groups and individuals living in multicultural Britain experience everyday life, be that in their workplace, the shopping centre or the local youth club. Romanians living in London tried to use anti-Roma discourses to separate themselves from the criminalizing assumptions underlying UK-based reporting on the end of transitional controls because they feared Romania's very place in the EU was being threatened. What has become apparent in the time since our research is that for many people and communities in Britain, such discourses have underpinned a growing sense of the need to separate the UK from the European Union, as the only way to prevent the challenges that migration has been discursively constructed as presenting.

## Notes

1. *KentOnline*: "KCC leader [ … ] set for thousands of migrants from Bulgaria and Romania as working restrictions lifted", 1 January 2014. Accessed 22 June 2015. http://www.kentonline.co.uk/deal/news/county-set-for-influx-of-10736/
2. ibid.
3. Identity categories we use are those that arose during interviews, see the introduction to this Special Issue for a discussion of terms used.
4. After 3 months, when putting in a claim they become subject to a more stringent HBT and a "genuine prospect of work" test. To meet the requirements EEA nationals must pass the minimum earnings threshold, based upon paying National Insurance contributions for the previous three months.
5. The stereotype included pictures of "women in colourful traditional dress while begging with children" as noted by Guy (2003, 70).
6. BBC News: "Romanian and Bulgarian migration debate - views in Europe", December 18 2013. Accessed 15 June 2013. http://www.bbc.co.uk/news/world-europe-25429420 . The press examples are as cited in the BBC report.
7. 18 months later the dominant focus shifted from EU migration back to "refugees" and "asylum seekers" crossing the Mediterranean and the Balkans to reach EU countries.
8. The simplification of complex experiences of Roma populations contrasts with other reports addressing this theme nationally for example Glennie and Pennington (2013).
9. For example "Romania and Bulgaria have a fairly high number of people who identify themselves as Roma. There are thought to be an estimated 10 to 12 million Roma living in Europe. Estimates of the number of Roma in the UK vary widely from 100,000 to one million." (Kent County Council 2013)
10. For example "It is possible that nationals from Romania and Bulgaria who identify themselves as Roma will choose to migrate to Kent, but it is not possible to

estimate or model this due to a lack of reliable data. Should Roma communities from Romania and Bulgaria settle in Kent, it is possible that some will require more support and resources from public services, partly due to the background of discrimination and deprivation that some Roma people come from" (KCC 2013).

11. For example "Conversations with KCC officers [and others] have identified some concerns that Eastern European Roma children in Kent [ ... ] are becoming victims of trafficking, exploitation and prostitution" (KCC 2013).

12. BBC Kent Online: "Council leader in immigration impact report call", 10 April, 2013. Accessed 22 June, 2015. (http://www.bbc.co.uk/news/uk-england-kent-22101490)

13. See Varju and Plaut in this journal for the historical context for the lack of data.

14. *KentOnline*: "KCC leader [ ... ] set for thousands of migrants from Bulgaria and Romania as working restrictions lifted", 1 January 2014. Accessed 22 June 2015. http://www.kentonline.co.uk/deal/news/county-set-for-influx-of-10736/

15. *Mail Online*: "Exposed: What they DIDN'T tell you about new wave of migrants heading for booming Britain", 28 December 2013. Accessed 22 June 2015. http://www.dailymail.co.uk/news/article-2530503/Exposed-What-DIDNT-tell-new-wave-migrants-heading-booming-Britain.html

16. She also referred to the group including friends from Congo.

17. The interpreter was a white Slovak woman.

18. In earlier fieldwork on the Romanian border a woman reluctant to become involved in the cigarette trade said: "I don't want to gypsy myself by getting involved in trading cigarettes across the border"

19. In 2013 in Romania, DS, an educated businesswoman, suggested that Romania has a high population of Roma because they are more tolerant of Roma than other European nation-states. As Woodcock (2007) has argued, DS' comment reflects broader political discourses, framing the Roma as a "European problem".

## Acknowledgements

Many thanks to all research participants in Kent and London who were so generous with their time and willing to share their experiences and insights. We are grateful to our partners in the EUBORDERSCAPES research project for their intellectual engagement and to the two anonymous reviewers for their scholarly and constructive feedback.

## Disclosure statement

No potential conflict of interest was reported by the authors.

## Funding

This work was supported by EUBORDERSCAPES (Bordering, Political Landscapes and Social Arenas: Potentials and Challenges of Evolving Border Concepts in a post-Cold War World) [290775] funded by the European Commission under the 7th Framework Programme [FP7-SSH-2011-1] Area 4.2.1. The evolving concept of borders.

# References

Balibar, E. 2002. *Politics and the Other Scene*. London: Verso.

Brambilla, C. 2015. "Exploring the Critical Potential of the Borderscapes Concept." *Geopolitics* 20 (1): 14–34.

Bunescu, I. 2014. *Roma in Europe: The Politics of Collective Identity Formation*. Farnham: Ashgate.

de Certeau, M. 1984. *The Practice of Everyday Life*. Berkeley: University of California Press.

Clark, C., and E. Campbell. 2000. "'Gypsy Invasion': A Critical Analysis of Newspaper Reaction to Czech and Slovak Romani Asylum-Seekers in Britain, 1997." *Romani Studies*, series 5 10 (1): 23–47.

Fairclough, N. 1995. *Critical Discourse Analysis*. London: Longman.

Foucault, M. 1980. *Power/Knowledge (Selected Works Edited by Colin Gordon)*. Brighton: Harvester.

Glennie, A., and J. Pennington. 2013. *In Transition: Romanian and Bulgarian Migration to the UK*. London: Institute of Public Policy Research.

Gramsci, A. 1971. *Selections from the Prison Notebooks of Antonio Gramsci*. Translated by Quintin Hoare and Geoffrey Nowell Smith. Reprint. London: Lawrence and Wishart, 2010.

Green, S. 2013. "Borders and the Relocation of Europe." *Annual Review of Anthropology*, 42: 345–361.

Guillem, S. M. 2011. "European Identity: Across Which Lines? Defining Europe Through Public Discourses on the Roma." *Journal of International and Intercultural Communication* 4 (1): 23–41.

Guy, W. 2003. ""No Soft Touch": Romani Migration to the U.K. at the Turn of the Twenty-first Century." *Nationalities Papers: The Journal of Nationalism and Ethnicity* 31 (1): 63–79.

Guy, W. 2004. "Recent Roma Migration to the United Kingdom." In *Roma Migration in Europe: Case Studies*, edited by W. Guy, Z. Uherek, and R. Weinrova, 165–210. Münster: Lit Verlag.

Guy, W., Z. Uherek, and R. Weinrova, eds. 2004. *Roma Migration in Europe: Case Studies*. Münster: Lit Verlag.

Johnson, C., and R. Jones. 2014. "Where is the Border?" In *Placing the Border in Everyday Life*, edited by R. Jones, and C. Johnson, 1–11. Farnham: Ashgate.

Johnson, C., R. Jones, A. Paasi, L. Amoore, A. Mountz, M. Salter, and C. Rumford. 2011. "Interventions on Rethinking 'the Border' in Border Studies." *Political Geography* 30: 61–69.

Jones, R. 2014. "Border Wars: Narratives and Images of the US-Mexico Border on TV." In *Placing the Border in Everyday Life*, edited by R. Jones, and C. Johnson, 185–204. Farnham: Ashgate.

Kent County Council. 2013. The Potential Impact on Kent Public Services of the Ending of Transitional Restrictions on Bulgarians and Romanians: Final Report October 2013.

McCall, L. 2005. "The Complexity of Intersectionality." *Signs: Journal of Women in Culture and Society* 30 (3): 1771–1800.

Nygaard, Christian, Adam Pasierbek, and Ellie Francis-Brophy. 2013. *Bulgarian and Romanian Migration to the South East and UK: Profile of A2 Migrants and Their Distribution*. Report prepared for the South East Strategic Partnership for Migration. University of Reading.

Philo, G., E. Briant, and P. Donald. 2013. *Bad News for Refugees*. London: Pluto Press.

Poole, Lynne, and Kevin Adamson. 2008. *Report on the Situation of the Roma Community in Govanhill, Glasgow*. Galsgow: Oxfam.

Pusca, A. 2010. "The Roma Problem in the EU." *Borderlands* 9 (2): 1–17.

Rumford, C. 2008. *Cosmopolitan Spaces: Europe, Globalization, Theory*. New York: Routledge.

Sigona, N., and N. Trehan, eds. 2009. *Romani Politics in Contemporary Europe: Poverty, Ethnic Mobilization and the Neoliberal Order*. London: Palgrave Macmillan.

Vaughan-Williams, N. 2008. "Borderwork Beyond Inside/Outside? Frontex, the Citizen–Detective and the War on Terror." *Space and Polity* 12 (1): 63–79.

Woodcock, S. 2007. "Romania and Europe: Roma, Roma and Tigani as Sites for the Contestation of Ethno-National Identities." *Patterns of Prejudice* 41 (5): 493–515.

Yuval-Davis, N. 2013. "A Situated Intersectional Everyday Approach to the Study of Bordering." EUBORDERSCAPES Working Paper 2 August 2013.

Yuval-Davis, N., G. Wemyss, and K. Cassidy. Forthcoming. *Bordering*. Cambridge: Polity Press.

# Press discourses on Roma in the UK, Finland and Hungary

Nira Yuval-Davis, Viktor Varjú, Miika Tervonen, Jamie Hakim and Mastoureh Fathi

**ABSTRACT**
This article analyses the political and media discourses on Roma in Hungary, Finland and the UK, in relation to the local Roma in these countries as well as those who migrated from Central and Eastern Europe countries following the fall of communism. The authors have analysed left of centre and right of centre major newspapers in these three countries, focusing on specific case studies which were the foci of public debates during the last two decades. We also examined a common case study in 2013 ("blond Maria") that was discussed throughout Europe. In each news paper, the constructions of Roma, local and migrant, and the changes to related discourses over the period were studied. In conclusion, we examine the multi-layered processes of social and political borderings in Europe which dominate discourses on Roma, "indigenous" and migrant, and the extent to which they constitute a coherent "European" construction of "the Roma".

## Introduction

In much of the literature on racism, colour and religion are constructed as the most important signifiers of racialization. And yet it is the Roma people who have emerged repeatedly in various studies as the most stigmatized and racialized grouping in Europe (Aluas and Matei 1998; Levine-Rasky, Beaudoin, and St Clair 2014). Following the expansion of the European Union (EU) in 2004 and the inclusion of Romania and Bulgaria in 2007, the diverse Roma groups can be seen as forming the largest ethnic minority within EU boundaries (ERRC 2010).[1] This article analyses the political and media discourses on both migrant and local Roma in Hungary, Finland and the UK, as illustrative of

105

the range of histories and policies to which Roma people have been subjected to in different parts of Europe.

As elsewhere in Europe, these countries have long-standing ethnic group-ings that contemporarily come under the umbrella name of Roma.[2] All these groups have underwent histories of persecution and racialization, as well as post-war policies ranging from forced assimilation and multicultural recog-nition. There are an estimated 650,000 Roma (Bernát 2014) living in Hungary who are diverse, but usually seen as composed of three main com-munities. The largest is the Hungarian-speaking Romungro, while the Vlach (Oláh in Hungarian) speak Hungarian and Lovari, and the Beás/Boyash Hun-garian and Romanian (Kemény 2000).[3] In Finland, the *Kaale* Roma are conven-tionally estimated to number around 10,000 individuals, with an additional 3,000–4,000 living in Sweden after migrating in the 1960s–80s (The Ministry of Social Affairs and Health 2009). In the UK there are around 400,000–500,000 Roma (Brown, Scullion, and Martin 2013, 7). It is a heterogeneous population with different cultural identities and lifestyles. The major older groupings are the Gypsies (British Roma), Irish Travellers, the "New Age Travellers".

In Finland and the UK, there has been a migration from Central and East European Roma communities since the fall of the Soviet Union, with arrivals of first asylum seekers, and later EU migrants. Despite the tiny size of the migrant groups in Finland and in the UK, their arrival has reactivated anti-Gyp-syist phobia of racialized "nomads",[4] and produced at times full-fledged moral panics. In the UK, the immigration of Irish Travellers has also been a debated issue. Meanwhile, in Hungary, the debates have dealt rather with the *emigra-tion* of Roma, with conflicting explanatory narratives pointing either to pro-blems within the Roma communities, within the Hungarian society as a whole or to external actors such as the EU.

This article examines press discourses both in relation to the "indigenous" Roma and those who migrated from and to these countries following the fall of communism in Central and Eastern Europe. In this, the article contributes to a growing body of literature on the situation of Roma in contemporary Europe (e.g. Sigona and Trehan 2009; Vitale and Legros 2011; Grill 2012; Picker 2016; Ryder, Cemlyn, and Acton 2014) as well as specific media and press studies (e.g. Clark and Campbell 2000; Bernáth and Messing 2013; Balch and Balaba-nova 2016). The main focus of our analysis is on the ways in which these press discourses on Roma have been used to construct bordering processes to differentiate between those who belong and those who do not.

## Methodology

The analysis in this article is embedded in the theoretical and methodological framework developed by the Work Package 9 team of the EUBorderscapes project on situated intersectional everyday bordering (Yuval-Davis 2014; Yuval-Davis, Cassidy, and Wemyss 2017). Our point of departure is a shared understanding of borders – social, political, geographical – not as territorial, static, naturalized, social and political "lines", but rather as continuous, dynamic and contested processes (e.g. Rajaram and Grundy-Warr 2007; Brambilla 2015). We further argue, that these bordering processes need to be understood as grounded in differing social positionings. We have thus sought to combine the methodological tools of what McCall (2005) calls inter-categorical and intra-categorical analyses, by exploring the shifting and contested constructions of the categories of analysis across space, time and normative political approaches.

We chose to apply these types of analyses to the press coverage of Roma/bordering issues because the mass media continues to be a key site in which forms of knowledge struggle to achieve the status of "common sense" (Gramsci 1971). As Edenborg (2016) argues, the media, by controlling and constraining visibility of particular groupings in particular ways, plays a crucial role in the construction, reproduction and contestation of borders and boundaries in specific political projects of belonging.

We began the analysis with a preliminary examination of the press in the three countries, focusing on several generic analytical categories reflecting the construction of Roma in the studied newspapers. These were discourses, categories and stereotypes used to describe and/or racialize the Roma; the extent to which all Roma were homogenized or differentiated into sub-categories; and the ways in which they were positioned vis-a-vis other ethnic minorities as well as the hegemonic majority in the country. We were further interested in whose voices were heard in the press discourses, and especially the extent to which Roma voices were included, if at all.

We analysed discourses on Roma in one left of centre and one right of centre newspaper in each country, at particular moments of time during the last two decades. In Hungary, the analysis focused on the left of centre *Népszabadság* (*NSZ*), and the right of centre *Magyar Nemzet* (*MN*), both daily newspapers. In Finland, we analysed coverage in the largest circulation newspaper *Helsingin Sanomat* (*HS*) and the evening tabloid *Iltalehti* (*IL*).[5] In the UK, the newspapers selected were *The Guardian*, a left of centre daily broadsheet and the right of centre *The Sun*, the largest circulation daily tabloid in Britain.

In each country, we measured the amount of yearly coverage of Roma issues in the left of centre newspapers to identify "peaks" of interest. The stories that produced these peaks became the case studies in this article. We also chose one common case study, "blond Maria", the girl seized by the police in Greece in 2013 from Roma people on suspicion of kidnapping.

In Hungary, using the Parliament Library database, we found a total of 2,719 news items on Roma groups in *NSZ*. The items given the most coverage were (1) a housing issue relating to thirteen Roma families in Székesfehérvár

107

(in 1997–98);[6] (2) a news story relating to a number of Roma families' migration from Zámoly and their refugee claims in Strasbourg (2001)[7] and (3) coverage of increasing racism and attacks against Roma (2009).[8]

In Finland we identified 965 relevant articles in *HS*. The three identified peaks related to: (1) the arrival of Roma asylum seekers from Slovakia, Poland, Latvia and Kosovo (1999–2000);[9] (2) debates on Finnish Roma culture, initiated by Roma activists and artists (2007)[10] and (3) debates on the circular EU-migration of Roma from Romania and Bulgaria, and on a legislative initiative to criminalize begging (2010–12).[11]

In the UK we identified more than 3,000 articles in *The Guardian*.[12] The identified peaks were (1) the increase in Czech and Slovak Roma migration to Dover in 1997;[13] (2) the Conservative Party's use of Roma issues in their 2005 election campaign which corresponded to a public campaign against "illegal" Roma squatters initiated by *The Sun*[14] and (3) the highly publicized eviction of a Roma community from the land they owned in Dale Farm, Essex in 2011.[15]

Exceptionally we also added a fourth UK case study focused on the remarks that ex-Home Secretary David Blunkett made about the alleged tension that Roma migrants were causing in Sheffield in 2013,[16] as this happened around the same time of the debate on the issue of "blond Maria".[17]

In the following, we report our main findings regarding the constructions of Roma, and how these have changed over the studied period. In the concluding discussion we examine the multi-layered processes of social and political borderings between the hegemonic majority and Roma, "indigenous" and migrant, paying also attention to the extent to which we can observe a "European" construction of "the Roma".

## The Hungarian case study

Although most of the Roma in Hungary belong to three main linguistic and cultural groups, the press discourse homogenizes and racializes them into a single subject. While stereotypes and discourses on Roma have been changing over the period we analysed, Roma remained a homogenous category in the press coverage. The only significant difference made in the press between the Roma is either specifying where they live in Hungary or from which countries they have migrated from and to.[18]

In 1997–98 the main Roma-related issue in the press was the so-called Székesfehérvár story. The local government of Székesfehérvár decided to demolish a run-down blockhouse where Roma were living and move them into container houses, then into cheap houses in the surrounding area of the city. This policy encountered fierce opposition from a Roma civil rights organization and people living in the local neighbourhood. In the eventual solution, the mayor agreed to settle the Roma in rented flats in the city rather than container houses. Meanwhile, the local people prevented the settlement of Roma families in the neighbouring villages.

The story of Zámoly,[19] which also began In 1997, became a hot issue in the press in 2000. Roma families were forced to leave their rented accommodation, which had been condemned by the local government as a result of storm damage. They were first settled into public housing, then moved into other settlements and finally, several years later, the National Roma Government[20] built wooden houses for them in Zámoly. However, the evacuated Roma families did not want to move into these houses, because of their fear of racism from the local population. Finally, led by a former local Roma representative, the families migrated to Strasbourg and claimed political asylum.

Both of these cases focus on the issue of adequate social housing as well as the racialized fear that local people have of the Roma moving into their neighbourhoods. In both cases the main public debates were around who was responsible for the issue, what caused it and who should provide the solution. While *MN* blamed the Roma in these stories, *NSZ* focused on the solution. This difference can be seen in the titles of the coverage.[21] The rhetoric of discrimination – with political context – was strong in the Zámoly case in 2001, especially in *NSZ*, as a critique of the Orbán government's Roma policy.

The analysis of the press during the peak in Roma coverage in 1998–99 reveals a contestation between a construction of Roma issues as part of "standard" social problems such as quality of life, housing problems, segregation and discrimination and a specific discourse focusing on "minority rights" for Roma. However, in relation to the latter, it was often argued that the Roma are more privileged than other Hungarian "official" minorities, or even the hegemonic majority. This argument was iterated particularly in relation to the Roma representation in the Hungarian Parliament, with conflicting arguments. In the *NSZ*, the ombudsman of minority rights (16 February 2009) voiced concern over everyday racism towards the Roma. A week later (25 February 2009) *MN* made an interview with the ombudsman, challenging his position: "Does defence of ethnic rights mean that only minorities have rights? Does the majority of the society have ethnic rights?"

The "Anti-Ghetto Committee",[22] established in 1989, is usually referred to as the starting point of Roma self-organization. During the following decade, a number of Roma politicians appearing in the public media faced accusations that this was mainly a strategy to advance their political careers. The "career-building" stereotype was often cited, especially by the right wing newspaper in the Zámoly migration (and the former Székesfehérvár housing) cases,[23] in relation to the families' leader, József Krasznai. He acted as a Roma representative also in the Székesfehérvár housing issue. As the story became a political issue on a national level, several other Roma representatives became involved and were subsequetly also vilified for it in the *MN*.

During the 2000s, the appearance of Roma people, leaders and politicians decreased significantly in the press. At the same time, there were routine referencing of Roma organizations and a number of former Roma representatives in mainstream politics. However, by the end of 2000s, discourses on the Roma had underwent a significant change. While there was a strengthening of radical right wing and incidences of lethal violence against the Roma, the media representation of the Roma became more heavily tinted by racism and criminalization of the Roma.[24] The rhetoric of the two newspapers, however, were quite divergent. While *NSZ* continued to problematize anti-Gypsyist racism and violence, *MN* constructed a racialized boundary of belonging between Roma and non-Roma people in Hungary:

> There are two types of society in Hungary today. People in the first know the rules of living together … The second society skipped the socialization, persons in it live on their instincts … most of the members of the second society are Roma. (*MN*, February 2, 2009)

Most of the press coverage on Roma relates to local Roma or, at times, their emigration from Hungary to France, Canada and the UK.[25] However, there are some articles that relate to Roma also in other Central and East European countries, discussing their migration to the West as a result of an all-European racism against Roma.[26]

However, the case of "blond Maria" did not fall into this category. It received little press in Hungary and when it was covered, the people involved were described as Bulgarian as opposed to Roma or Bulgarian Roma.[27]

Overall, the discourse on Roma in the Hungarian press seems to be directly connected to wider public debates and party and governmental politics. The stories about the Roma are often used to highlight the failed general politics and/or Roma policies of the political party the newspaper opposes, whether on the right or left of the political spectrum (although, as a rule, *NSZ*'s discourses were more moderate than those of *MN*).[28]

Everyday Romani people's voices are under-represented in the analysed articles. Most of the time they were represented by Roma local government officials, human rights organizations and the minority ombudsman. There is a clear decline in the representation of Roma voices in the press. While in 1998, the voice of at least one Roma is present in about half of the analysed articles, in 2009, it had decreased to about a quarter.

Roma groups are constructed, especially but not exclusively in the left wing *NSZ*, as both part and outside of Hungarian national society. Their emigration is viewed as an outcome of this racialized ambiguous belonging, both by the local Roma and by the hegemonic Hungarian collectivity. While *NSZ* is more sympathetic to the plight of the Roma, and *MN* tends to discredit their grievances, this perspective is shared by the two newspapers.

## The Finnish case study

Throughout the analysed Finnish material, a consistent distinction is made between the national Roma minority and the Roma migrants from Eastern Europe. The discourses on the former connect to a long history of problematizing the Finnish Roma as a domestic "other", but also to the increasingly sensitive rhetoric of modern minority politics (Tervonen 2012). There are thus evident tensions and shifts in what can and should be written in relation to the Finnish Roma, as exemplified by the rapid replacement of the ethnonym *mustalainen* ("Gypsy") by *romani* ("Roma") in the 1990s.[29] During the public debates Finnish Roma culture in 2007, there is also a discernible element of cautiousness in most of the writing in the *IL* and the *HS*.[30]

Meanwhile, debates on the migrant Roma are connected to a politicization of humanitarian and low-skilled immigration, and have clearer continuities with old anti-Gypsyist and racial discourses. A narrative of borders threatened by unwanted newcomers is particularly clear in relation to the mostly Slovakian asylum seekers who arrived in 1999–2000. Despite a recognition of discrimination and human rights violations,[31] they are nevertheless not considered as "real" asylum seekers.[32] Both papers specify the Roma ethnicity of the migrants from the start, with *IL* evoking exoticizing stereotypes of dark-eyed wanderers.[33] In the substance of the editorials and op-eds, there is no significant difference between the newspapers.[34] A hierarchy is built between "real" asylum seekers and the "uncontrollable torrent" of arriving Roma, and the authorities are presented as "unable to manage the situation" because of overly liberal asylum laws.[35] The migrants are pointed to as an argument for more restrictive asylum policy. Both *IL* and *HS* voice support for the authorities' urge for stricter legislation.[36] When a temporary visa requirement on Slovakian citizens was imposed, this was termed "inevitable" by both papers,[37] and greeted by the *IL* as a "solution" to "the problem of Roma arriving to the country".[38]

In comparison, the debate on the EU migrants and the begging ban in 2010–12 brings to the surface more political contestation and critical discussions. There is a division into "pro" and "con" editorials and columns, and corresponding conceptualizations of the Roma migrants as either "victims"[39] or "criminals".[40] The "victim" perspective, representing the Roma migrants as structurally discriminated against, recurs particularly in the *HS*,[41] and occasionally in the *IL*.[42] The EU is implicated; for example, an op-ed published in 2010 argues that "the Roma who flee from a vicious cycle of poverty are the flipside of the European integration process – an image of European poverty painful to look at".[43] However, the conclusions drawn from the victim perspective vary, with the idea that "they should be helped in their home countries" used to argue against inclusive policies in Finland.[44]

From 2012 onwards, the discourse on the "Roma beggar" seems to become less ethnicized and lose some of its urgency. The volume of writing in *IL* and *HS* decreases; in a number of articles the situation of EU migrants is written of as part of wider migration-related policy issues, concerning, for example, access to health care,[45] homelessness[46] or politics of free movement in Europe.[47]

There are no direct references to "race" (*rotu*) in the studied texts, and little explicit references to anti-Roma stereotypes. The distinction between domestic and foreign Roma means that there is no straightforward lumping together of all Roma into one racialized group. However, *within* the main groups written about, there is little internal differentiation. Particularly, the asylum seekers are written about as a singular homogenous group, constituting a "Roma problem".[48] Moreover, particularly in *IL*, "neutral" news items are frequently coupled with headlines, images and captions which play more directly with racialized stereotypes. The Roma migrants are also implicitly or explicitly associated with crime in almost a quarter of the *IL* coverage studied. With no ethno-specific crime statistics, such implicit association can be created for example by collapsing the categories "Roma" and "Romanian", and presenting crime statistics on the latter to delegitimize the former.[49] Meanwhile, unsubstantiated references to human smugglers and Mafioso organizers of begging rings appear also in the *HS*.[50]

The most direct racial references occur in *IL* related to "blond Maria". Between 18 and 26 October, a series of articles created a moral distinction between dark-skinned child kidnappers on the one hand, and police, child care agents and Nordic parents of missing children on the other. *IL*'s piece on 18 October ("Has she been kidnapped from Scandinavia? A blond girl found in a Roma camp") cites Greek police and portrays Maria's host parents as kidnappers and/or human traffickers.[51]

*HS* was more cautious and started publishing more on the case only after evidence started mounting against the initial narrative of child-snatching Roma. Still, also in *HS* there was a persistent ethnic framing of the reporting, with the Romani ethnicity of the host parents/kidnapping suspects mentioned in every article on the issue.[52]

Overall, there is a consistent difference with regard to Finnish Roma and Eastern European Roma migrants in *HS* and *IL*. The Finnish Roma are given a relatively more positive and diffuse coverage. While NGO representatives and "ordinary" Finnish Roma are frequently given voice, Roma migrants are seen and discussed but seldom heard. The discourse is dominated by authorities, with human rights NGOs as a countervoice.

*IL* and *HS* differ particularly in their approach to the migrant Roma, with *Iltalehti* more prone to associate the migrants with crime and to play on racialized stereotypes in its use of images and headlines. Still, both newspapers seem to be characterized by a tendency towards surface-level "neutrality" in avoiding expressly racialized language; while oscillating between "victim" and "criminal" perspectives; and relying heavily on the authorities as a source of information. To the extent that wider immigration dilemmas are discussed via the case of the Roma migrants, then, the discursive "bordering out" follows in the Finnish case a distinctively governmental logic.[53]

## The UK case study

The major finding from the UK data is the way in which different Roma groups are homogenized in order to function as a sign onto which anxieties around perceived threats to the law abiding "British way of life" are drawn, whether in terms of anti-nomadism or in terms of the perceived threat of the EU to the UK's sovereignty and territorial integrity. This projection is achieved through the deployment of a multiplicity of discourses such as welfare, planning policies, cultural traditions, racial constructions and human rights. These discourses change emphasis in relation to different case studies but all relate in some way to an EU policy being introduced to the UK. The overall effect is the "othering" of these different Roma groups.

In 1997, the major discursive framework used to make sense of the recently arrived Roma in Dover is that of welfare. This is achieved through the persistent use of three related discursive figures: the gypsy beggar, the welfare scrounger and the bogus asylum seeker.[54] The Sun constructs these figures in its own voice whereas The Guardian critiques The Sun and other right wing newspapers for doing so as part of its coverage.[55] The policy background at the root of the anxieties being projected onto the Roma in this news story, is the Dublin Convention's attempt to standardize asylum processes across the EU.

The Sun uses the terms Czech, East European[56] and Gypsy[57] interchangeably with homogenizing effect. The Guardian's coverage constructs a pro-migration, anti-racist reader/self.[58] The "other" is the sympathetically portrayed persecuted Roma. This othering is softened somewhat by the inclusion of quotes from Czech Roma teenagers.[59] These quotes, however, often reinforce racial stereotypes.[60] The self in The Sun is the hard-working taxpayer who is opposed to the "chancers" and "con-merchant" Gipsies [sic] who are falsely claiming asylum in order not to work but to scrounge off the welfare state. In a Sun political cartoon an alien representing Czech and Slovak Gipsies [sic] lands at the foot of the white cliffs of Dover asking "Take me to your … benefits office".[61]

In 2005 the press discourse focuses on the legality of the traveller's way of life. Issues of public spending remain significant though are secondary to the legal questions raised. The policy background to this story is the incorporation of the European Convention on Human Rights into British law. Both the

Conservative campaign and *The Sun* accuse the travellers of abusing the new legislation.[62] *The Guardian* uses its principles in the traveller's defence.[63]

The Roma in this story are homogenized as an "invasion"[64] or a "plague" for example.[65] At the same time an important distinction is made between the "real" "good" Roma, living in authorized sites and "fake" nomadic travellers.[66] Exceptionally, the settled communities are aligned with the British self which, in *The Sun*, is described in various places as "law abiding",[67] "hard-working citizens",[68] "peaceful"[69] and as "tax-payers".[70] There are no "good" Roma in *The Sun*'s coverage of the other stories. The "bad" Roma other is constructed as privileged in comparison to the hard-working British tax-paying citizen, exploiting as well as breaking the law,[71] benefiting from state services that "ordinary" citizens are not entitled to.[72] Significantly many of the "bad" Roma are identified as being of Irish origin, who escaped to the UK in order not to comply with the caravan legislations there.

The Dale Farm story concerns a long-running legal debate over an Irish Traveller community's right to live in an encampment on land they had owned for ten years but did not get planning permission to do so, as their site was seen as a threat to the surrounding community. *The Guardian*'s coverage of the eviction was both nuanced, sympathetic in tone and included a range of different views including that of the travellers. Nevertheless it still deploys the racially objectifying discourses historically associated with the right wing press, primarily depicting Dale Farm as squalid.[73] *The Sun* adopted a different representational strategy, depicting Dale Farm as a site of both undeserved privilege for the travellers that live there and as a drain on state resources.[74]

The Sheffield story focuses on the moral panic generated by David Blunkett's[75] remarks which appeared to suggest that the worst imaginable outcome of the easing of migration to the UK from Romania and Bulgaria is the arrival en masse of Roma from these countries.[76] Discursive frameworks of law and welfare do not disappear entirely from this story but they are superseded by explicitly racialized discourses in both newspapers.

*The Guardian* does this in a contradictory fashion. While it published an explicitly anti-racist feature,[77] it also published an in-depth feature from the anti-Gypsyist perspective of a multi-ethnic vigilante group who police the streets of Sheffield.[78] The effect is a peculiarly racialized construction of a super-diverse, yet still racist, British self, constructed against an homogenized, potentially criminal Roma migrant Other. *The Sun* reproduces the same discourses but includes even more crude racial stereotypes of the recent Roma migrants. They are "filthy".[79] They have "reputation for industrial-scale begging and theft".[80] They also attempt to sell babies to multicultural shop owners.[81] Interestingly, unlike in previous years, *The Guardian* offers no space for Roma voices while the *Sun* does include a Roma voice in its coverage.[82] This pattern repeats itself also in the "blond Maria" story.

In the UK coverage of the "blond Maria", discourses of biological constructions of race predominate almost entirely, focusing on hair colour and skin pigmentation.[83] In *The Sun*, crude representations of Roma portray them as fairy tale villains, swarthy child snatchers who force children to dance for money and enter into forced marriages.[84] *The Guardian*'s coverage is more nuanced and reflexive, running a range of different types of feature on the story, including an opinion piece by a self-identified blond Roma man.[85] Despite the heavily racialized construction in both papers, they both also refer to how economically and racially discriminated Roma are, *The Guardian* more so than *The Sun*.[86]

In the main, then, *The Guardian* has tended to have more self-reflexive and multidimensional coverage than *The Sun*. However, throughout this historical period *The Sun* appeared to set the news agenda, with *The Guardian* often reacting to it and other right wing tabloids. At the beginning of the period *The Guardian* included more Roma voices in its coverage and was more sympathetic to their situations than *The Sun*. In 2013 *The Guardian* allows space for fewer Roma voices and produces more troublingly racialized representations of Roma. *The Sun* consistently produces cruder racial stereotypes of different Roma groups throughout.

During this period two clear trends of change develop in Roma representations across both newspapers. Firstly, different Roma groups are frequently constructed as a sign onto which anxieties re EU policies that are perceived as threatening Britain's sovereignty and territorial integrity are projected. Secondly, in the unfolding of this process, a multiplicity of discourses the general trend has been a move towards a racialized representation that assigns Roma groups a fixed inferior identity similar to the (post-)colonial representation of black and Asian people. As such, it is implied, they can never belong to British society.

## Concluding discussion

This examination of discourses of both "left" and "right" main stream newspapers in Hungary, Finland and the UK has clearly shown that Roma people have been racialized and "othered" in all three countries, although the historical specificity of each country means that these discourses are constructed around differing policies, practices and everyday borderings.

An essential part of these racialized discourses is the process of homogenization. Although in the UK and Hungary the "indigenous" Roma belong to more than one cultural and linguistic group, these differences do not usually appear in the media narratives. While country of origin might be specified, in Finland and the UK, the two countries with migrant Roma, the only significant distinction made is between the local and the migrant Roma. This duality overlaps with a more or less subtle distinction made between the "good" and the "bad" (or "accepted" and "problematic") Roma, and works to reproduce racialized discourses on the alleged criminality of the latter.

The discourses on the Roma are caught in the basic ambivalence of the politics of belonging which are applied, in somewhat different ways in different countries, towards the local Roma. Even when constructed as part of the national citizenship body, they are consistently framed as being apart. The recognition of their "otherness" operates both as a means of collective empowerment and self-representation and as means of exclusion, hierarchization and discrimination. In Hungary, we can see in the different case studies the effects of the shifts in policies and practices towards the Roma where, during the Soviet period, forced assimilation policies were enacted to obliterate ethnic distinctiveness and mobile livelihoods. The post-Soviet period saw the rise of self-representation and governance of Roma, but these policies of collective recognition were placed in a socio-economic context of rising unemployment, collapsing public housing and rising racialized violence that acted as a major factor pushing Hungarian Roma towards emigration as well as transnational travel to Western countries.

In Finland, the press discourses reveal racialization of the immigrant Roma, who appear overwhelmingly as anonymous and problematic "others". Meanwhile, belonging and citizenship of the members of the national Roma minority are rarely questioned, and the press discourses towards them are characterized by an increasing sensitivity and even cautiousness. Still, they are persistently framed as ethnically distinctive "special cases".

Racialization and othering in the UK have been operating in different ways towards local and migrant Roma. The exclusionary discourses towards the former are often connected to anti-Gypsyist stereotypes of dangerous "nomads". Unlike in Hungary and Finland where post-war transformations forced Roma to find permanent housing, major sections of UK Roma continue to live in mobile homes. Although British multicultural policies have been aimed at migrants from the former empire,[87] British traditions of patronage, acceptance of and provision for different ways of life were applied also towards the Roma, requiring local councils to provide official caravan sites where Roma could collectively live. This provision was never sufficient in space and often lacked appropriate amenities of education and health and with the neo-liberalization of the British state the legal space available to Roma became progressively more scarce. Much of the debates in the press, as in the Dale Farm case, focused on the criminalization of all those who could not or would not live on these sites, including those who managed to buy private land and wanted to live there on their own terms.

The similarities as well as differences in the construction of everyday borderings towards Roma in the three countries are expressed in the different extent to which they participate in the public media discourses concerning them. In Hungary, Roma voices are heard, but usually only those few who are considered the official representatives of the Roma community, especially around the period in which Hungary joined the EU and had to demonstrate a positive human rights record.[88] In Finland, members of the national Roma minority frequently appear in texts concerning them; while the Roma migrants are continuously discussed but rarely heard. In the UK, there is less differentiation in this sense between local and migrant Roma but the ratio of their voices being allowed to be part of the media representation is the lowest of all.

An interesting difference between the ways Roma are racialized in the different countries came to light in the case study of the "blond Maria" examined in the press of all three countries. In Hungary the Bulgarian Roma involved were constructed as Bulgarian seasonal workers. In Finland and even more so in the UK, the narratives of the press involved shift from a racialized culturalist construction of the Roma into a biological one.

Overall, our case studies from three highly divergent contexts make it clear that Roma are constructed as "Others" in shifting and contested, yet highly persistent ways. While we found significant differences in discourses towards "indigenous" Roma and migrant Roma, these differences go hand in hand with the general direction in which constructions of social and political borderings have been developing in Europe towards Roma in recent years which affect all Roma, migrant or not. These changes can be linked to more general changes in European politics of belonging, the rise of "autochthonic" constructions of belonging (Yuval-Davis 2011) and the neo-liberalization of the relationships between civil society and the state.

The racialization and criminalization of Roma migrants serve, however, also another purpose. They have become a rhetoric and illustrative devise for those in western European countries, and particularly in Britain, who fear free movement of people within the expanded EU. The moral panics concerning migrant Roma, as described in the press of all three countries, are closely associated with the more general anxieties connected to westward mobilities from Central and East Europe (as well as from the global South). In Finland and the UK, the Roma are constructed as the most problematic or even dangerous of the Eastern European migrants. As a result, additional bordering practices concern the attempts of non-Roma migrants from these countries to differentiate themselves from the Roma so as not to be conflated with them.[89] Most significantly, these migrations, as a result of the expansion of the EU and vital for its neo-liberal economy, have undermined the sense of closure and security of "Fortress Europe" and reinforced xenophobic movements all over Europe that refuse to recognize EU citizens as entitled to national welfare provisions.

The most alarming – although not surprising – finding of our comparative study is that with time, the trajectories point towards increasing racialization and criminalization, with more exclusion and less collective recognition. The

2013 biological racialization discourse of the "blond Maria" case in Finland and the UK, unlike the more culturalist one used in most of the articles discussing the Roma during this period, is a sobering reminder that racialized discourses usually encompass, rather than simply substitute, earlier hegemonic ones.

## Notes

1. While an estimate of eight to twelve million Roma people in Europe is often cited (e.g. Tanner 2005), other estimates vary between four and fourteen million, pointing to a substantial uncertainty about the category (Guild and Carrera 2013, 4–7).
2. As in the rest of the special issue we use the term Roma as a generic term while being aware of the multiple and contested labels in which the subject of the analysis in this article are named by themselves and by others.
3. This distinction is rare, however, both in the media and in the scientific literature.
4. We are using the term anti-Gypsyism following the Special Report by Izsák (2015) for the Human Rights Commission.
5. As is the case with all the largest newspapers in Finland, both *Helsingin Sanomat* and *Iltalehti* are politically independent and formally non-aligned.
6. *NSZ*: 67 articles (38 news, 13 features, 1 letter, 15 op-ed); *MN*: 19 (11 news, 3 op-ed, 5 features).
7. *NSZ*: 73 articles (57 news, 10 op-ed, 6 features); *MN*: 60 articles (36 news, 7 features, 4 letters, 13 op-ed).
8. *NSZ*: 126 articles (79 news, 27 features, 20 op-ed); MN: 72 articles (37 news, 2 letters, 14 features, 19 op-ed).
9. *HS*: 148 articles (82 news, 13 letters, 10 op-eds/editorials, 43 features). *IL*: 31 articles (21 news, 1 editorials, 4 letters, 5 features).
10. *HS*: 47 articles (17 news, 9 op-eds/editorials, 11 letters, 10 features). *IL*: 6 articles (3 news, 1 letter, 1 editorial, 1 features).
11. *HS*: 149 articles (77 news, 14 op-eds/editorials, 23 letters, 35 features). *IL*: 24 articles (19 news, 5 features).
12. The Nexis database used to find these articles cannot return more than 3000 search results.
13. *The Guardian* had 16 articles (10 news, 6 letters), *The Sun* 11 articles (7 news, 12 op-ed).
14. *The Guardian* – 24 articles (14 news, 1 letter, 7 op-ed, 2 features); *The Sun* – 64 articles (47 news, 4 letters, 12 op-ed).
15. *The Guardian* – 50 articles (33 news, 4 letters, 8 op-ed, 5 features); *The Sun* – 111 articles (90 news, 16 op-ed, 5 features).
16. *The Guardian* – 11 articles (6 news, 5 op-ed). *The Sun* – 13 articles (9 news, 4 op-ed).
17. The articles which appeared in October 2013 relating to the "blond Maria" story in the newspapers we studies in the three countries were Hungary – no articles in *MN*; 3 in *NSZ*.
    Finland: 13 in *IL* and 7 in *HS*. The UK: 12 in *The Guardian* (8 news, 4 op-ed); 23 in *The Sun* (22 news, 1 op-ed).
18. For example, Roma from Mohács (and often from Miskolc) who often migrated to Canada, were identified as "Canadian" Roma.
19. Village in Hungary.

20. "National Roma Government" was organized as an NGO, representing Roma on national level, the "official" partner of the government in Roma issues.
21. *MN*: "Obsession of 'Fehérvár'"; *NSZ*: "Radio street: the story of a compromise". November 29, 1997.
22. It was established in February 1989, in Miskolc and is seen as "the starting point of Roma self-organisation Roma civil right movement" (*NSZ*, Februray 21, 2009).
23. For example, " ... the behaviour of the leader of local minority government is very close to corruption ... István Hell, József Krasznai ... and Aladár Horváth (*Roma representatives*) tried to make political capital unfairly in the period of election" (by another former Roma representative: *MN*, January 10, 1998).
24. Cf. Bernáth and Messing (2013).
25. For example, "They came back" *MN* May 15, 2009.
26. For example, "Asylum seeking" *NSZ* June 8, 2009.
27. *NSZ*, short articles on October 22, 23, 25 and 26, 2013
28. eFor example, "French refugee status for Zámolyans" *NSZ*, January 6, 2001. "Two politicians from the opposition (left-wing, MSZP) went to Strasbourg to meet with Roma migrants and discuss their main problems (to make political benefit from the situation)" *NSZ*, March 14, 2001; "We should see how this campaign was organised: these people departed from a small village and arrived into the middle of the EU. It would be worth to ask: Who paid for the whole action?" *MN*, January 10, 2001.
29. The word "mustalainen" practically disappears in HS but appears occasionally in *IL*; for example, in a story published 27 October 1999, *IL* refers to Romani culture throughout, but concludes that there are approximately 10,000 "mustalaista" in Finland.
30. Yet, individual articles particularly in the *IL* portray Roma "cultural rules" as a source of problems, alleged to cause difficulties in allocating public housing, family feuds and discrimination against women, for example. *IL* August 25, 2007; *IL* January 10, 2009.
31. For example, *IL* July 2,1 999; *IL* July 5, 1999, *HS* June 30, 1999.
32. *IL* July 5, 1999.
33. For example, referring to the flights taken by the asylum seekers as "wandering" or "nomadism" (*vaellus) Romanien kansainvaellus, IL* July 5, 1999; or, to childlike migrants with "dark eyes" and to the Emil Kusturica movie *Queen of the Gypsies*; (*IL* June 30, 1999).
34. Cf. *IL* July 7, 1999; *HS* July 7, 1999.
35. Citation from *HS* July 7, 1999; compare to the article on the same day in *IL*.
36. The two newspaper use strikingly similar rhetoric derived from the authorities. According to the IL, "The world's refugee problem is not solved by opening the borders of Finland; and it is doubtable whether those in the biggest need of help ever even appear on our airports" (*IL* July 5, 1999). Meanwhile, *HS* claims the "Law has to be changed quickly" and that "The loopholes in the present law do not serve anyone's interests, least of all of those in genuine need for an asylum. The welfare refugees enabled by the present law only stoke xenophobia" (*HS* July 7 1999).
37. *IL* July 7, 1999; *HS* July 7, 1999.
38. *IL* July 7, 1999.
39. For example, *HS* December 7, 2009; *IL* July 9, 2013.
40. For example, *IL* June 20, 2011; *HS* March 22, 2008.

41. An early example of this dominant narrative in HS is a story titled "The Roma are victims above all" (*HS* January 14, 2008).
42. *IL* July 9, 2013.
43. *HS* August 20, 2010.
44. As stated by an MP interviewed by *HS*, December 21, 2010. Besides discrimination, a victim perspective is evident in articles which consider the arrival of first the asylum seekers and later EU-migrants as a result of a hoax by organized criminals, who "tricked the Roma in order to make money". For example, *IL* July 8, 1999; *HS* November 27, 2009.
45. For example, *IL* March 18, 2014; *HS* March 8, 2014.
46. For example, *HS* September 4, 2014.
47. For example, *HS* May 24, 2014.
48. For example, "Roma problem" solved by Visa restriction (*IL* July 7, 1999); "Roma problem" requires European efforts (*HS* October 12, 2010).
49. *IL* June 20, 2011.
50. For example, *HS* March 22, 2008.
51. On 19 October, *IL* shifted focus to Maria's neglected state, praising the "safe children's home" she's was admitted into. While the conditions provided by her host parents are described as "crammed and unhygienic", no worry is expressed for the children remaining in these conditions who were *not* blonde and blue-eyed. *IL* October 18, 19, 22, 24, 25 and 26, 2013.
52. The same was true of the two subsequent Irish cases: the focus was on ethnicity rather than on poverty or child welfare. In contrast to national reporting, *HS* and *IL* referred to "the Roma", whether the context was Ireland, Greece or Bulgaria.
53. For example, *HS* January 6, 2000.
54. *The Sun* October 21,1997; *The Sun* October 24, 1997; *The Guardian* October 22, 1997.
55. 22 October 1997.
56. 22 October 1997.
57. 28 October 1997.
58. 22 October 1997; 25 October 1997.
59. 13 November 1997.
60. "Yes, we're noisier and more temperamental, but that's the way we were born. When I celebrate my birthday, I like to drink and sing, but the Czechs find that hard to deal with" Arnost Kotlar, roma. (ref).
61. 23 October 1997.
62. 23October 2005.
63. 17 March2005.
64. *The Sun* March 21, 2005.
65. *The Sun* March 22, 2005.
66. *The Sun* March 10, 2005.
67. 21 March 2005.
68. 14 March 2005.
69. 11 March 2005.
70. 19 March 2005.
71. 11 March 2005.
72. 14 March 2005.
73. "On an island of gravel surrounded by a sea of mud, Michelle Sheridan closes her caravan door against the stench of raw sewage and makes a cup of tea" (4 November).

74. 26 September 2011.
75. A former Labour government minister.
76. Race row boiling in borderless Britain; "LABOUR WARNS OF TENSION ... "(17 November 2013 – 28 and 29).
77. 18 November 2013.
78. 16 November 2013.
79. 17 November 2013.
80. 30 December 2013.
81. 15 November 2013.
82. 17 November 2013.
83. *The Sun* October 23, 2013; *The Guardian* October 21, 2013.
84. 22 October 2013; 24 October 2013.
85. 26 October 2013.
86. *The Guardian* October 22–25, 2013; *The Sun* October 24, 2013.
87. What used to be known as New Commonwealth Countries or Pakistan (NCWP) countries.
88. For ways in which these formal voices have been challenged please see the article by Scott et al. in this issue.
89. See the paper by Cassidy and Wemyss in this issue.

## Disclosure statement

No potential conflict of interest was reported by the authors.

## Funding

This work was supported by EUBORDERSCAPES - Bordering, Political and Social Arenas: Potentials and Challenges of Evolving Border Concepts in a post-Cold War World, Call identifier: FP7-SSH-2011-1, Project Number: 290775..

## References

Aluas, J., and L. Matei. 1998. "Discrimination and Prejudice: Minorities in Romania." In *Scapegoats and Social Actors: The Exclusion and Integration of Minorities in Western and Eastern Europe*, edited by Daniele Joly, 101–111. Basingstoke: Macmillan.
Balch, A., and E. Balabanova. 2016. "Ethics, Politics and Migration: Public Debates on the Free Movement of Romanians and Bulgarians in the UK, 2006–2013." *Politics* 36 (1): 19–35.
Bernát, A. 2014. "Leszakadóban: a romák társadalmi helyzete a mai Magyarországon." [Lagging Behind: The Social Situation of Roma in the Recent Hungary]. In *Társadalmi Riport* edited by T. Kolosi and Tóth I. Gy. 246–264. Budapest: TÁRKI.

Bernáth, G., and V. Messing. 2013. *Pushed to the Edge. Research Report on the Representation of Roma Communities in the Hungarian Mainstream Media, 2011*. Budapest: CEU CPS.

Brambilla, C. 2015. "Exploring the Critical Potential of the Borderscapes Concept." *Geopolitics* 20 (1): 14–34.

Brown, P., L. Scullion, and P. Martin. 2013. "Migrant Roma in the United Kingdom: Population Size and Experiences of Local Authorities and Partners." University of Salford. Accessed August 28, 2015. http://www.salford.ac.uk/__data/assets/pdf_file/0004/363118/Migrant_Roma_in_the_UK_final_report_October_2013.pdf.

Clark, C., and E. Campbell. 2000. "'Gypsy Invasion': A Critical Analysis of Newspaper Reaction to Czech and Romani Asylum-seekers in Britain, 1997." *Romani Studies* 510 (1): 23–27.

Edenborg, E. 2016. *Nothing More to See: Contestations of Belonging and Visibility in the Russian Media*. Lund and Malmo: Lund and Malmo Universities.

ERRC (European Roma Rights Centre). 2010. Website. Accessed September 9, 2015. http://www.errc.org.

Gramsci, A. 1971. *Selections from the Prison Notebooks of Antonio Gramsci*. Translated by Quintin Hoare and Geoffrey Nowell Smith. Reprint, London: Lawrence and Wishart, 2010.

Grill, J. 2012. "Going up to England: Exploring Mobilities among Roma from Eastern Slovakia." *Journal of Ethnic and Migration Studies* 38 (8): 1269–1287.

Guild, E., and S. Carrera. 2013. "International Relations, Citizenship and Minority Discrimination: Setting the Scene." In *Foreigners, Refugees or Minorities? Rethinking People in the Context of Border Controls and Visas*, edited by D. Bigo, S. Carrera, E. Guild, 1–20. Farnham: Ashgate.

Izsák, R. 2015. *Comprehensive Study of the Human Rights Situation of Roma Worldwide, with a Particular Focus on the Phenomenon of Anti-Gypsyism*. Report to the Human Rights Council, June.

Kemény, I., ed. 2000. *A magyarországi romák* [Roma of Hungary]. Budapest: Press Publica.

Levine-Rasky, C., J. Beaudoin, and P. St Clair. 2014. "The Exclusion of Roma Claimants in Canadian Refugee Policy." *Patterns of Prejudice* 48 (1): 67–93.

McCall, L. 2005. "The Complexity of Intersectionality." *Signs* 30 (3): 1771–1800.

Ministry of Social Affairs and Health. 2009. *The Proposal of the Working Group for a National Policy on Roma*. Helsinki: Ministry of Social Affairs and Health.

Picker, G. 2016. "'That Neighbourhood is an Ethnic Bomb!': The Emergence of an Urban Governance Apparatus in Western Europe." *European Urban and Regional Studies* 23 (2): 136–148.

Rajaram, P. K., and C. Grundy-Warr, eds. 2007. *Borderscapes: Hidden Geographies and Politics at Territory's Edge*. Minneapolis: University of Minnesota Press.

Ryder, A., S. Cemlyn, and T. Acton, eds. 2014. *Hearing the Voices of Gypsy, Roma and Traveller Communities. Inclusive Community Development*. Bristol: Policy Press.

Sigona, N., and N. Trehan, eds. 2009. *Romani Politics in Contemporary Europe: Poverty, Ethnic Mobilization and Neoliberal Order*. London: Palgrave Macmillan.

Tanner, A. 2005. "*The Roma of Eastern Europe: Still Searching for Inclusion, Migration Information Source (May)*." www.migraitoninformation.org/feature/displace.cfm?id=308.

Tervonen, M. 2012. "Romanit ja suuri muutos'" [Roma and the Post-war Transformation]. In *Suomen Romanien Historia*. edited by P. Pulma, 166–197. Helsinki: Suomalaisen Kirjallisuuden Seura.

Vitale, T., and Legros, O. 2011. "Les migrants roms dans les villes françaises et italiennes: mobilités, régulations et marginalités." [The Migrant Roma in French and Italian Cities: Mobilities, Regulation and Marginality]. *Géocarrefour* 86 (1): 3–14.

Yuval-Davis, N. 2011. *The Politics of Belonging: Intersectional Contestations*. London: Sage.

Yuval-Davis, N. 2014. "Situated Intersectionality and Social Inequality." *Raisons Politiques* 58: 91–100.

Yuval-Davis, N., K. Cassidy, and G. Wemyss. 2017. *Bordering*. Cambridge: Polity Press.

# Index

9 780367 264857